# Corporate Chanakya
on Leadership

INCLUDES AUDIOBOOK READ BY TOM ALTER

SPMGROUP
SINCE 1967
SPM Foundation

Radhakrishnan Pillai

JAICO PUBLISHING HOUSE
Ahmedabad Bangalore Bhopal Bhubaneswar Chennai
Delhi Hyderabad Kolkata Lucknow Mumbai

Published by Jaico Publishing House
A-2 Jash Chambers, 7-A Sir Phirozshah Mehta Road
Fort, Mumbai - 400 001
jaicopub@jaicobooks.com
www.jaicobooks.com

© Radhakrishnan Pillai & SPM Foundation

CORPORATE CHANAKYA ON LEADERSHIP
With Audiobook
ISBN 978-81-8495-307-7

First Jaico Impression: 2012
Eighth Jaico Impression: 2018

No part of this book may be reproduced or utilized in
any form or by any means, electronic or
mechanical including photocopying, recording or by any
information storage and retrieval system,
without permission in writing from the publishers.

Printed by
Rashmi Graphics
#3, Amrutwel CHS Ltd., C.S. #50/74
Ganesh Galli, Lalbaug, Mumbai - 400 012
E-mail: rashmigraphics84@gmail.com

The book is dedicated to
My Gurudev Swami Chinmayananda,
who inspired me to study our ancient scriptures that
offer solutions to all our modern day problems.

Contents

Author's Note		ix
Preface		xiii
Chanakya — Who Was He?		xix
Acknowledgements		xxi

Power

1	Power in the Corporate World	3
2	Power Brings Responsibilities	5
3	The Art of Punishment	7
4	Staying at the Top	8
5	Create Your Own Law	11
6	Control Your Office	13
7	Leaders Have the Edge	15
8	Maintain Secrets	16

9	The Seven Pillars of Business	18
10	Three Aspects of Success	21
11	Power Management	23
12	Bosses Are Answerable	25
13	Applying *Arthashastra* in Business	27
14	Inherited Company	29
15	A Public Awakening	31

Qualities of a Leader

16	Total Alertness	35
17	Advice to Entrepreneurs	37
18	Multiple Tasking	39
19	Open-Door Policy	41
20	Ethics in Business	43
21	Start Now	45
22	Knowledge for a Leader	47
23	Decision Making	49
24	The Spiritual Side	51
25	An Eye for Detail	53
26	Being Energetic	55
27	Improve What You Inherit	57
28	Setting an Example	59
29	Work Through Problems	60
30	Respect and Protect Women	62

| 31 | Don't Forget Your People | 64 |
| 32 | Passing the Mantle | 66 |

Competition

33	Handling Competition	71
34	Army and Treasury	73
35	Protection From Enemies	75
36	Right Opportunity	77
37	Win-Win Policy	79
38	The Winning Weapon	81
39	Win the War	83
40	Win-Win Situation	85
41	The Key to Success	87
42	Game Theory	89
43	Winning Over Friends and Foes	91
44	Respect Your Enemies	93
45	Strategy vs Tactics	95
46	Before You Attack	97
47	Aspects of a Battlefield	98
48	Partnership Among Equals	100
49	A Safe Retreat	102
50	In the face of Competition	104
51	Acquiring a Company	106
52	Where to Expand	108

| 53 | Peace and War | 110 |
| 54 | Tackling Terrorism | 112 |

People

55	Growing Under a Mentor	117
56	Motivating Employees	119
57	Bidding Goodbye to Employees	121
58	Managers into Leaders	123
59	Delegating Work	125
60	Protecting Old Employees	127

To Avoid

61	What a Leader Should Not Do – 1	133
62	What a Leader Should Not Do – 2	135
63	What a Leader Should Not Do – 3	137
64	What a Leader Should Not Do – 4	139
65	What a Leader Should Not Do – 5	141
66	What a Leader Should Not Do – 6	143
67	What a Leader Should Not Do – 7	144
68	What a Leader Should Not Do – 8	147
69	What a Leader Should Not Do – 9	149
70	What a Leader Should Not Do – 10	151

Author's Note

The journey of *Corporate Chanakya* has been encouraging beyond belief. For a debut author, writing the first book itself was a challenge. But seeing it grow into a national bestseller has been more than a dream come true! The team at Jaico did a fantastic job of publishing and distributing the book.

As a leadership trainer, I have been travelling across the globe teaching at various universities, business schools, corporates and government organisations. The media consistently carried fantastic reviews for the book. It has been heartening to always see it on the 'Most Recommended' or 'Best Sellers' shelves in bookshops.

Inspired by the book, Shemaroo, the entertainment company made *Chanakya Speaks*, an 'edutainment' film now ready for launch. It is the world's first business management film on Chanakya. During the making of the film, Shemaroo came up with the idea — an audio book on *Corporate Chanakya*.

Tom Alter, the veteran Bollywood actor and theatre and television artist, agreed to do the voice over. I am personally thankful to him for taking the book to another level altogether.

The book *Corporate Chanakya* had 3 sections – Leadership, Management and Training. During one of my training programmes, the Chairman of the company who was attending the program said, "Your book has 3 books within it!" I discussed the possibilities with Jaico, of bringing out *Corporate Chanakya* as 3 individual books on Leadership, Management and Training. And about giving voice to each of them!

So here you have in your hands *Corporate Chanakya on Leadership*, a single volume containing 70 chapters. And it comes along with an audio CD book that you can listen to, as you read! I highly recommend both, because revision only makes a student perfect. But do not forget to apply what you have learnt! Practise the theory. Act on the ideas. Implement your plan...

An Overview:

• Chanakya, Kautilya, and Vishnugupta are the names of the same person. Either of the names has been used in this book to refer to Chanakya.

• This book does not compare Indian management ideas against western management ideas. In fact it is complementary to western management thoughts. We have taken the best of both worlds.

• In most cases, leaders have been referred to as 'he'. But it also applies to 'she' as well. Since Chanakya has taken the King (male gender) as the leader, the pronoun 'he' is used. Leadership and management skills are not gender-based but they are qualities which can be developed as a 'mind-set'.

• In this book, I have referred to verses or *sutras* from *Kautilya's Arthashastra*. For those who would like to read the verse in the original text, the verse number is written in brackets. The first digit is the book number. The second is the chapter number and the third digit is the verse number. For example,

"He (leader) should constantly hold an inspection of their works, men being inconstant in their minds." (2.9.3)

So, this verse is from *Kautilya's Arthashastra* Book 2, Chapter 9 and Verse 3. The same format has been followed in all chapters.

• The book that readers can refer to for the verses quoted, is the English translation of *Kautilya's Arthashastra* by R.P. Kangle of Mumbai University, published by Motilal Banarasidas. The explanations given are the interpretation of the author. Various other translations and commentaries of *Arthashastra* other than this book are available.

TIP

This book has 70 chapters. The idea is not to read it as a novel but to enjoy its practical benefits. Read a chapter, or a few chapters, a day, apply the teachings in your life, and observe the benefits. It only takes three minutes to read each chapter.

Go ahead – Discover the Chanakya in you!

Preface

LET ME TELL you a story...

There was once a young man in Mumbai who wanted nothing more than to succeed in the world of business. He had studied management in colleges that extolled the virtues of the western ways of understanding this subject. Soon enough, he worked his way up the corporate ladder, but finally decided to set out on his own. After all, who wants to be bossed over by someone else?

His first venture was in the realm of spiritual tourism. Since no one in his family had ever been an entrepreneur, he had to learn everything about setting up a business on his own. By the grace of God, and the support of his business partner, the business began to do well. From being a manager in someone else's company, he had become the leader of his own business.

His next step? Creating a well-known corporate entity. He met people and discussed his ideas and plans with them, learning from people, making copious notes, reading books, attending seminars, and training programmes. And yet, nothing helped. Something vital was missing in his pursuit for knowledge. He was not able to figure out what this missing piece was, for a long time.

The answer was right within him.

Since his childhood, he had found guidance in a spiritual organisation and had been blessed by many spiritual masters. During a spiritual discourse a Mahatma said, "India, our motherland, has great history and legacy. Our *Rishis* were no ordinary men — they have studied and perfected every science in this world. Only if we were to look back into our glorious past we would find solutions to all our modern problems."

This was the divine message he had been waiting for.

Management has been recognised as a science since the 1950s. One of the fathers of modern management is Peter Drucker. But didn't 'management' exist in India even before the 1950s and the Drucker era? As a nation we have over 5000 years to our credit. Did we not have management scientists in our country before the 20th century?

In the ancient Indian scriptures — *Ramayana, Mahabharata,* the various *Upanishads* — he found brilliant discussions of management strategies. Why was it that we Indians, always look at what is *wrong* with India and never appreciate what is *great* about our country? As a nation we have survived the test of time. Even though we are still a growing economy, we are not a failed nation. In the past, our country had achieved the peak of success for thousands of years. How many nations can boast of such a heritage?

He now realised that the missing piece which would help his business grow was to look 'within' rather than outside. The western principles of management are undoubtedly good, but even his own ancestors were extremely good at management.

Thus, one day, while looking for Indian books on management, he stumbled upon *Kautilya's Arthashastra*, written by the kingmaker, Chanakya. Who has not heard about this book? Even he had. But hardly anyone from his generation had studied it. He bought a copy.

A few pages into the book, he was upset! He could not understand anything! He read the pages over and over again, but the message of the book was out of reach. The subject itself seemed dry and boring. He felt the author had made everything seem more complicated than necessary.

He said to one of his mentors, "I do not understand anything in the *Arthashastra*, even though I am trying my best to learn from it." His mentor told him, "In India, we consider the scriptures to be mirrors. They reflect who you are. So if you do not understand *Arthashastra*, do not blame the mirror. As you grow and experience life, you will understand the book better."

That year, he went on a pilgrimage to Kailash Mansarovar, the holy abode of Lord Shiva. One evening, a voice seemed to speak to him, 'Make *Kautilya's Arthashastra* your lifelong pursuit. Don't just study it, but apply it in your life. Live the *Arthashastra*!' He could not believe that he was listening to his *own* thoughts, this had to be divine intervention!

He had heard about an ashram in Kerala, dedicated to the

research of ancient Indian scriptures. He declared to the Acharya (teacher) in charge of the ashram, "I want to study the *Arthashastra.*" The Acharya was happy to see the young man's interest, but said, "You will have to come here and learn it under the Guru-Shishya Parampara." This meant taking a break from the business and staying in the ashram and studying under a Sanskrit scholar.

This was not an easy decision for a businessman from Mumbai. But, with the help of his partner, he took time off from the business, and studied the wisdom of the Rishis. The time he spent in the ashram changed his life forever.

He realised that each modern management theory had already been explored thousands of years ago in the *Arthashastra.*

With a deeper knowledge of management he now returned to his urban life to apply what he had learned. Immediately, he experienced success! His business grew and people were impressed with his new skills. When they asked him how he had achieved success, he said, "Two things helped me — the grace of my Guru and the knowledge of *Kautilya's Arthashastra.*"

Friends, this is my story. Every word is true. But, the story does not end here. In fact, this is where the story begins....

After I returned from Kerala I applied Kautilya's practical and perfect theories to my own business (Atma Darshan, *www.atmadarshan.com*). Even though Atma Darshan brought me success, something else began to happen. My friends from the corporate world urged me to share this knowledge I had gained.

I was invited to speak at various seminars, conferences, and training programmes in India and all over the world. Businessmen consulted me on several matters. Well-known publishing houses and newspapers asked me to write about how Kautilya's wisdom could be applied to modern businesses. I was also asked to host a radio show.

I met so many people who are interested in Indian management and Indian wisdom. Despite the differences between them with regard to age, nationalities, designations, and industries, all those who participated in my workshops and chose to attend my seminars felt a deep respect for Chanakya's genius.

And then came the support of the SPM Group of companies which allowed me to delve deeper into *Arthashastra*. I am now fully devoted to the cause of the promotion and application of Indian management ideas. Today, I am the Director of the SPM Foundation which aims to 'make India strong and self-sufficient' in the ancient Guru–Sishya Parampara method.

This book is a documentation of all my ideas that I have shared with millions of people from the corporate world, all across the globe, about how to apply Chanakya's practical solutions to solve day-to-day problems in modern businesses.

Corporate Chanakya on Leadership is not just about me. It's about you and everyone else who wants to practise the principles of Indian Management in their work and wants to be successful.

Chanakya
Who Was He?

BORN IN 4TH CENTURY B.C. in India, Chanakya was also known as Vishnugupta and Kautilya. Through the centuries, scholars have described Chanakya as a rare mastermind who became an expert in varied and specialised fields like management, economics, politics, law, leadership, governance, warfare, military tactics, accounting systems, and several others. The 6000 *sutras* have been classified into 15 books, 150 chapters, and 180 topics by Chanakya himself.

He was responsible for bringing down the Nanda dynasty and establishing his able student Chandragupta Maurya on the throne as the Emperor. Hence, he is called a 'Kingmaker'. He is also credited with masterminding the defeat of Alexander in India who was on his march to conquer the world.

As a political thinker, he was the first to visualise the concept of a 'nation' for the first time in human history.

During his time, India was split into various kingdoms. He brought them all together under one central governance, thus creating a nation called 'Aryavartha', which later became India. He documented his lifelong work in his book *Kautilya's Arthashastra* and *Chanakya Niti*.

For ages, rulers across the world have referred to the *Arthashastra* for building a nation on sound economics, based on spiritual values.

Arthashastra when literally translated means 'scripture of wealth' but it contains knowledge about every subject under the sun. It's the knowledge of wealth and a wealth of knowledge.

Acknowledgements

WHEN I STARTED on my journey to learn and teach Chanakya's ideas I was not sure about how it would work. It was just an idea, a dream. I took my first step and then thousands of well-wishers joined me and encouraged me along. The number of people who are responsible for making this book a reality is endless. I must acknowledge some of these wonderful people who gave me strength right from the start.

Chinmaya Mission

I am a 'product' of the spiritual organisation Chinmaya Mission (*www.chinmayamission.com*). I met my Gurudev Swami Chinmayananda (1916-1993) when I was a child. He is my spiritual and management guru. Gurudev said, "A single ideal can transform a listless soul into a towering leader among men." This statement has been the guiding principle of my life.

Today, Swami Tejomayananda, the global head of Chinmaya Mission, continues to give me the same support. He chose the beautiful name of my first company — Atma Darshan (vision of the self).

Among hundreds of Acharyas (teachers) of the mission, some with whom I am closely associated require mention — Swami Sacchidananda, Swami Sadananda, Swami Ishwarananda, Swami Swaroopananda, Swami Mitrananda, have encouraged me to spread the work of Chanakya.

Swami Advayanandaji — the Acharya in charge of Chinmaya International Foundation (CIF) accepted me as a student of CIF where I learnt the complete 6000 *sutras* of *Arthashastra* and this has been the turning point in my life.

Dr. Gangadharan Nair, former Dean of Adi-Shankara Sanskrit University, Kalady, Kerala, my teacher and my guru of *Arthashastra*. His wife, Dr. Uma Devi Nair, herself a Sanskrit scholar, was like a mother to me while I was studying the *Arthashastra*.

Venkat Iyer, my friend since childhood and later my partner in the company Atma Darshan. Without his support, I couldn't have spent time learning about Chanakya's work. He also runs a successful venture called Wealth Tree Partners (*www.wealthtree.in*).

Muulraj Chheda and SPM Group, came as a godsend. Muulraj, is the Director of Swati Energy and Projects Private Ltd, part of the SPM group of companies. SPM stands for Strength, Progress with Maturity, and is also the initials of the three Founder brothers — Shantilal, Pravin, and Mavji Chheda. They supported my research and promotion of Chanakya's works.

Today, I am the Director of SPM Foundation (*www. spmfoundation.in*) the education wing of SPM Group (*www. spmgroup.co.in*) the vision of which is to bring back ancient Indian knowledge and apply it to our modern day problems. The other directors of the SPM Group — Rajen Chheda, Kinnjal Chheda, Niket Shah, Guruvinder — and their spouses have supported me in my search of knowledge. Each day, when we sit for lunch together, I call it my 'classroom' where words of wisdom from senior members have always given me insights into the intricacies of human nature.

MTHR Global, is More Than HR Global (*www.mthrglobal.com*). The core team — Rajesh Kamath, Vipul Agarwal, Ashish Gakrey, Rajesh Gupta, and Preeti Malhotra — were the first to christen me *Corporate Chanakya*. I dedicate the title of this book to them.

Mumbai University's Dr. Shubhada Joshi, Head of Department of Philosophy, and her team, gave my work on Chanakya the academic outlook it required. SPM Foundation partnered with the Mumbai University for offering joint programmes on 'Chanakya's Management Ideas and Indian Philosophy'.

Worldspace Satellite Radio's Karthik Vaidyanathan, Harish Puppala, Seetal Iyer came up with a wonderful idea for a show called 'Ask Chanakya' on Moksha, a channel on Worldspace. I hosted at least a hundred shows.

Also, I am grateful to my other 'media friends' — Dinesh Narayan, Meenal Bhaghel, and William Charles D'Souza for their support.

Gautam Sachdev promoter of (*www.indiayogi.com*) introduced my first online e-course based on *Arthashastra*.

My course now has students from over 25 different countries. I am glad that I can use technology to take Chanakya's message to the world.

Several Management Gurus supported my thirst for knowledge. I would like to thank Dr. Subhash Sharma, Dr. M.B. Athreya, Debra and William Miller, Sudhir Seth, and Dr. Anil Naik.

I am grateful to the Police Force — Sandeep Karnik, (IPS) Dhanraj Vanzari, Milind Bharambe (IPS), Satish Menon (Railway Protection Force) — who made me realise that behind the tough looking cop there is a human being who feels just like you and me.

My family, especially my parents, C.K.K. Pillai and Sushila Pillai, have my heartfelt gratitude. Coming home late at night, not being sure of a regular income while I developed a business, missing weekends and family time while prioritising professional commitments, my life would never have been smooth without my wife Surekha. Her parents Shekhar and Dhanvati, and her sisters Sarikha and Chandrika bring joy to my life.

My First students of Arthashastra — Mala Thevar, Yogesh Sanghani, Anuraag Gupta, and his sister Seema Gupta, and Anupam Acharya. Their dedication to knowledge has given me the confidence that this good work will continue for many long years after I am gone.

And I must thank Ranjit Shetty, my friend from the Chinmaya Mission, who has decided to dedicate all his time to implementing the ideas of Chanakya.

Power

1

Power in the Corporate World

THE CORPORATE WORLD'S search for supremacy over competitors and players from other industries can be summed up in one phrase — the search for power. All CEOs refer to this struggle for power as though it was warfare strategy. No wonder then that the book *The Art of War* by Sun Tzu is often quoted by various CEOs in their strategy plans.

Kautilya's Arthashastra is India's contribution to the subject of warfare strategy. From the 15 books in *Arthashastra*, six books are dedicated to the art of warfare. A deep study of these chapters will give us an insight into the factors that contribute to the making of a powerful organisation.

Kautilya outlines the various factors that lead to true power.

- Intellectual Power

The power of knowledge. The corporate world is today led by knowledge workers. It's the intangible asset of any organisation. Management gurus across the globe are talking about the knowledge revolution that is sweeping through this century. The greatest commodity in the future will be 'knowledge'. No wonder then that the richest man in the world, Bill Gates, is part of the IT industry which is *only* knowledge-oriented. Even the highest paid executives are evaluated on the basis of the knowledge they have gained over the years.

- Man Power

Men are the assets of an organisation. There are two kinds of manpower — internal and external. Internal manpower comprises employees of the organisation, the board of directors and the shareholders. External manpower includes the customers and suppliers. It is because of them that we exist. We have to focus on satisfying our customers. As Peter Drucker, the father of management, points out, "The aim of marketing is to know and understand our customers so well that the product or service fits them and sells itself."

- Financial Power

Financial success ensures the progress of an organisation. A sound balance sheet is the parameter on which employees, shareholders, and stakeholders continue to give their support to the organisation. As Jack Welch, the former Chairman of GE points out, "Nothing succeeds like success." To be financially successful is very essential. It gives a lot of courage to the organisation to not only share its profits, but to also reinvest it in various productive areas like research and development, venture into new projects and ideas, and contribute to social causes.

- Power of Enthusiasm and Morale

This is the most important factor of all. A leader who is charged with enthusiasm and a high level of morale can create the other three factors. Research has proved that the most productive organisations are the ones that create a very high energy level. The drive to 'get more' is the true sign of progress. Venturing into new markets, scaling high targets, working towards deadlines… all find their roots in enthusiasm. All great organisations have inspired leaders.

2

Power Brings Responsibilities

ALL OF US REMEMBER the ideas and ambitions we would write about in school essays on topics such as, 'If I were the Prime Minister of India'. We would imagine a utopian society and how we would run it. Smartly carving our solutions to fit socio-economic, political and security related problems, we could write about the ideal society endlessly.

But is it easy to get and remain in power? Is it secure and safe to remain at the top?

About the dangers a king has to face, Chanakya says:

"For the king, there is (danger of) revolt in the interior or in the outer regions." (8.2.2)

The greatest danger for a king is revolt. This is what he has to be wary of and protect himself from. What does 'revolt' mean to a business leader? It means dissatisfied employees, shareholders, and stakeholders, who are integral elements of the organisation. There are also external threats from suppliers, customers, and clients.

Even politicians know that if they do not rule the country properly, the dissatisfied voters can overthrow them.

How can you keep everybody happy when you are in command of an organisation?

- Understand The Needs Of The Market

As a leader, it is important for you to understand the needs of the people in the organisation, as well as in the market and the industry. As long as you are fulfilling their needs, they will be loyal. But while carrying out a 'Needs Analysis' you should also be able to differentiate between need and greed.

- Remember Old Clients While Making New Ones

Business is not a onetime deal, but a collection of deals over a period of time which makes the business successful. Hence, understanding the requirements of people around you is a continuous process. You should always be on the move. Keep meeting your old clients regularly even when you are in the process of expanding your client base.

- Solve the Problem Immediately

To curb any revolt, early action is must. Similarly, it is necessary to curb the dissatisfaction of the employees and clients, the moment any issue crops up. When you sense any threat in terms of market or labour unrest, pay attention to the problem and resolve it as soon as possible.

A good leader knows that only committed employees run an organisation. They also are aware of the fact that only satisfied customers bring good business.

3

The Art of Punishment

THE CEO, OR THE LEADER, of any organisation has a tough role to play. In order to reach the target set by the board of directors he has to tactfully get the work done by his team. Dealing with the employees is not an easy task. He has to consider their problems, understand where they are stuck, and solve their problems immediately so that work does not suffer.

At the same time, he has to be a disciplinarian. He should be very flexible with the employees, but he should not lose focus of the goals and priorities of the organisation — the reason for which he has been appointed.

At times, he has to even use a rod (punishments) to discipline his employees. How much punishment can be given, when it can be given, and why — is an art in itself. This art is perfected by Kautilya in the *Arthashastra*. This is one of the reasons why *Kautilya's Arthashastra* is also called *Dandaniti* — the art, or the strategy, of punishments.

Are punishments required at all? Can an organisation or leader do without it? Punishments are carried out if one steps out of the framework that are laid down in any society or organisation. This is because stepping beyond the framework is harmful for everyone. But, what if this framework has not been laid down?

"If the rod is not used at all, the stronger swallows the weak in the absence of the wielder of the rod." (1.4.13-14)

The leader or the CEO is the final authority in the matter of punishments. If he is not disciplining his team from time to time, there is always the possibility of him being seen as a poor leader. More importantly, in his absence, the law of the jungle will take over and disturb the setup and structure of the organisation. The 'bully' in the team will start overpowering the weak as he would not be afraid of the boss, or the actions that will be taken when he returns.

However, the CEO should not just punish employees for the sake of showing off his power and position.

"The king severe with rod (punishment) becomes a terror. A king with a mild rod is despised. The king just with the rod is honoured." (1.4.8-10)

He will become like Hitler if he is too severe and unfair. At the same time, if he is too soft, people will take him for granted. The leader who knows the right level of punishments, carried out in the right manner and at the right time is always respected. He is honoured by one and all. Such a disciplined leader is highly productive.

4

Staying at the Top

IT IS EASY TO GET to the top, but it's very difficult to stay there. Once you are in the leader's position, the whole dynamics of the game changes. The priority now is to get everything right and maintain your position.

Kautilya was aware of this truth and hence, guides leaders about how to avoid one's downfall, as well as that of the organisation.

He points out:

"Control over the senses, which are motivated by training in the sciences, should be secured by giving up lust (Kaam), anger (Krodha), greed (Lobha), pride (Mana), arrogance (Madh), and overexcitement (Harsha)." (1.6.1)

A leader is carefully watched by each person around him. Apart from the external observers, like the media and intelligence agencies, his team members are also watching every move he makes. All his subordinates look to him as their role model. Such a leader should be very careful in his private as well as public life.

As Stephen Covey says in *Seven Habits of Highly Effective People*, "Private victory leads to public victory."

A leader's success is maintained by controlling the senses. For this, Kautilya pointed out the following six negative behaviours that need to be avoided:

- Lust (*Kaam*)

Lust is the deep hunger for any object which results from over-attachment. People at the top level are carried away by the lust for power. That is why it is recommended that they should identify the new leaders and train them. Leaders should slowly evolve into mentors guiding the new generation to take over.

- Anger (*Krodha*)

Maintaining a cool head is very essential. A short-tempered leader is neither appreciated nor liked by his team members. Such a person is very unpredictable. One should be able to control oneself in all circumstances, most importantly in public.

- Greed (*Lobha*)

Gandhiji had rightly said, "There is enough in this world for every person's need but not enough for one man's greed." Satisfaction does not mean complacency. One should be dynamic, yet not get carried away by purely material gains. He should also focus on the social and spiritual contributions he can make.

- Pride (*Mana*)

Even when at the top, a leader should be able to initiate more and more projects. However, a feeling that "I am the doer" should not be entertained. He should understand that, after all, his success is because of teamwork. A highly egoistic leader is sure to lose his team members in the long run.

- Arrogance (*Madh*)

An arrogant leader will always take the credit for every success, while he blames failures on others. Instead, he should share the results of success with everyone. His motto should be, "It is 'we' who have succeeded not 'I'."

- Overexcitement (*Harsha*)

A leader should never get overexcited. Expressing extreme happiness or sadness has to be avoided. When the whole world is on fire, it is only the one with a balanced mind who can find a solution.

5

Create Your Own Law

IN SANSKRIT, 'LAW' IS called *dharma* — meaning that 'which holds'. For example, what holds people onto planet earth? It's the 'law' of gravity. If this law was missing, then everything would be out of control.

Similarly, in every home, organisation, and country, a certain law exists that holds everyone together. In most cases, like in our homes, these laws are unwritten, yet practised. While in organisations and countries, they are documented as rules, regulations, constitutions, mission statements, etc.

Here, Chanakya suggests that if the laws have not been set down in an organisation, the king (the leader) should take the lead in setting them down:

"When all laws are perishing, the king here is the promulgator of laws, by virtue of his guarding the right conduct of the world consisting of the four varnas and four asramas." (3.1.38)

So, if you are the leader of an organisation, you have to take the lead in laying down the rules too. But, before you do that, keep the following in mind:

- A Law for What?

The first question one needs to answer is, why do I require this new law. Until this is clear, we will just be creating something mechanically without any clarity of what we are achieving.

In some companies where I conducted a 'goal-setting' workshop, I found that rule-setting was merely a formality, not something that 'they' really wanted from the depth of their hearts. Compliance issues and government rules are signed about the setting up of new companies without even knowing why these rules have to be followed. As a leader, it is important to have a clear 'vision' for the organisation.

- Benefit for All

Let's go back to the fundamental principle of *Kautilya's Arthashastra*. What is the duty of a king? "To consider the benefit of ALL his subjects and act accordingly." Therefore, when you are making a policy, take into consideration the benefit of all and not just that of your own. The welfare of all is the foundation on which we build a country, society, and any institute. If this is missing, then the subjects will be disappointed and, in the long run, will either replace their leader, or search for a new one.

- Fit for All

In the verse quoted here, Chanakya says that the king should make laws according to the four *varnas* and *asramas*. This means that we are looking at various, deeper aspects of subjects and workers — such as age, talents and natural qualities — while taking various decisions. For example, an economically poor person stealing a piece of bread may be let off unpunished, as for him the act of stealing was a matter of survival, rather than greed. This human perspective is important.

6

Control Your Office

THE OFFICE IS AN integral part of any organisation. Even in the past, it was compared to a fort — or *Durga* in Sanskrit. This was from where the king would rule. Keeping control of the fort was essential for the king.

This is no different from today's corporate world in which a CEO needs to keep control of his office.

Chanakya says:

"He should cause the treasury and the army to be collected in one place, in the fortified city, in charge of trustworthy men." (5.6.7)

This is the prerequisite of a good office.

But, let's look at each aspect of this 'office' in detail:

- Treasury

The head office is from where the treasury is monitored. Only if the treasury is well-managed, can other things be directly controlled. If the treasury becomes weak, problems crop up. Hence, it is essential to keep it full and protected.

- Army

An army includes all the employees — right from the CEO, to the peon and the driver. All of them form a complete unit. There's just no division in teamwork. Each person is equally important. When there is a war, or competition, each person should be able to deliver his best. Thus, a good office has good, talented, skilled, and capable men.

- Trustworthy Men

In every organisation there are key people who run the show. They are the lieutenants to the commander. Such people should be trustworthy and should also be able to trust others. These key positions — decision makers — are the backbone of any business unit.

So, in the above verse, the strategy according to Chanakya is that the the leader should control the treasury (finance) and the army (people) from one place — the fortified city (the office/plant) — and let trustworthy men (managers) run the show.

On achieving such a setup, the CEO or Director will have another advantage. The fact that all these components are under one roof makes them easy to monitor on a regular and continuous basis.

Now, since we are already talking in modern terms, let's understand one more thing — the office should also be well-equipped with the latest weapons. This means that the installed systems should be constantly upgraded, the technology should be the latest and the computers and other effective tools should be properly used.

But then, all these technical additions do not guarantee success. Just like in war, the success of any group or organisation depends on multiple factors. But in the end, success depends on the 'brains' of the leader.

As the former Indian Army Chief, General J.J. Singh puts it, "Finally, it is the man behind the machine, who makes you win the war."

7

Leaders Have the Edge

THE LEADER, THE CHIEF EXECUTIVE, or the Chairman of a company, has the most important role to play in taking the organisation ahead. Being at the helm, he has to guide the organisation and help it achieve higher goals and set new trends.

He has to ensure that the organisation is growing stronger, not only financially, but also in terms of the foundation and the value systems set in place by the founders and visionaries. The organisation has to grow from being just a profit-making machine to a contributor to society, an enterprise for the well-being of one and all. To achieve this, the leader has to lead by example.

How does Kautilya define an ideal leader?

"If the king is energetic, his subjects will be equally energetic. If he is slack (and lazy in performing his duties) the subjects will also be lazy, thereby, eating into his wealth. Besides, a lazy king will easily fall into the hands of the enemies. Hence the king should himself always be energetic." (1.19.1-5)

Being energetic is the most important quality of a leader. A self-motivated person, he has to raise the enthusiasm of his team members too. Only if he is energetic, will his employees be energetic too. If he is lazy, the employees will also lose interest in their work and very soon, a sense of complacency will take over the whole organisation.

All great leaders who have set a trend in the corporate world were highly motivated and inspired. The best example from recent times is J.R.D. Tata.

A visionary leader, JRD, as he was popularly known, was largely responsible for making Tata a trusted household name in the country. He not only guided the Group towards higher achievements and helped it grow, but he was also an important part of the process.

JRD was the first Indian to get a pilot license in his early twenties. He was responsible for setting up Tata Airlines — the first commercial airline in the country which is today Air India. The airline was the best in terms of punctuality, service, and efficiency. In Air India's golden jubilee year, JRD flew a solo flight between Mumbai and Karachi. He was always a leader who led from the front.

What if the leader is not very alert and active? With the high level of competition around it is easy for his enemies to overtake him. A slack leader will also cause the company he heads to become financially weak. Fundamentally, a leader should be physically active, mentally alert, and intellectually convinced.

Once Swami Chinmayananda, a great leader, who continued working even when he was very old, was asked, "Why do you go around doing so much work? Why can't you take rest?" Quick came the reply, "If I rest, I rust."

8

Maintain Secrets

A LEADER HOLDS A VERY responsible position in any team and hence, also in an organisation. He has to be very careful when he speaks and of the words he uses. If he utters a single, wrong statement it can destroy his organisation.

One of the important factors that a leader should know is how to maintain secrecy.

Kautilya warns the leaders,

"To as many persons the lord of men (the leader) communicates a secret; to so many does he become subservient, being helpless by that act (of his)." (1.8.9)

There are various projects and issues that the leader should never talk about openly. Until and unless it is the right time, he should not make these secrets publicly known.

Every project that is executed in an organisation goes through three stages — the conceptualisation stage, preparation stage, and delivery stage. At each stage, there are key 'secrets' that only a leader should know. He should never let others know these secrets.

What if he keeps telling others his secrets? Let's look at two possible repercussions:

- He Has to Bend Down

A leader has to bow down to all the people who know his secrets. If more people know his secret, the leader will have to bend down that much more. A leader should always be in control of the situation, and not allow others to control him. If he has said the 'right' thing to the 'wrong' person, he has to be at the mercy of that person who may not keep that secret. Such a person may not only blackmail him, but also leak the information to competitors and enemies.

- **He Becomes Helpless**

Having shared his secret with others, the leader becomes totally helpless. Instead of thinking about how to carry out his plans, he will worry about how to protect himself from attacks.

A golden rule in business is, think twice before you speak. Even a tailor is advised during his apprenticeship, "Measure twice, but cut once."

Kautilya's enemies were afraid of him because they could never understand what his next move would be. He always had multiple plans ready. If one plan failed, he was ready to attack with the next, totally surprising his enemies.

Chandrashekhar Azad, the Indian freedom fighter, was another person who was always a mystery to everyone. He would never allow anyone to know where he would go to next. Not only the British, but even his own team members, like Bhagat Singh, would not know his hideouts. He believed that he was 'Azad' — the ever free person. If he wanted to be truly free, he had to keep himself unknown to others.

Therefore to be free — keep your mouth shut!

9

The Seven Pillars of Business

A STRONG FOUNDATION IS THE key to any successful business. Your vision, your commitment, your purpose, all these form the all-important pillars of an organisation, the most essential part of any building.

In his groundbreaking *Arthashastra*, Chanakya lists the seven pillars of an organisation.

"The king, the minister, the country, the fortified city, the treasury, the army, and the ally are the constituent elements of the state." (6.1.1)

Let us now take a closer look at each of them:

- The King (The Leader)

All great organisations have great leaders. The leader is the visionary, the captain, the man who guides the organisation. In today's corporate world we call him the Chairman, Director, CEO, etc. Without him the organisation will lose direction.

- The Minister (The Manager)

The manager is the person who runs the show — the second-in-command in the organisation. He is also the person you can depend upon in the absence of the leader. He is the man who is always in action. An extraordinary leader and an efficient manager together bring into existence a remarkable organisation.

- The Country (The Market/Client/Customer)

No business can exist without its market capitalisation, its clients, and customers. The market is the area of your operation. The place from where you get your revenue and cash flow. You dominate this territory and would like to maintain your monopoly over this segment.

- The Fortified City (Head Office)

You need a control tower, a place where all plans and strategies are made. It's from here that your central administrative work is carried out. It's the nucleus and the center of any organisation.

- The Treasury

Finance is an extremely important resource. It is the backbone of any business. A strong and well-managed treasury is at the heart of any organisation. Your treasury is also your financial hub.

- The Army (The Team)

When we go to war, we need a well-equipped and trained army. The army consists of your team members. Those who are ready to fight for the organisation. The salesmen, the accountant, the driver, the peon — all of them add to your team.

- The Ally (Friend/Consultant)

In life you should have a friend who is just like you. Being in the same boat, he can identify with you and stay close if you need help. He is the one you can depend upon when problems arise. After all, a friend in need is a friend indeed.

Look at these seven pillars. Only when these are built into firm and strong sections can the organisation shoulder any responsibility and face all challenges. And while building them, do not forget to imbibe that vital ingredient called 'Values', speaking about which, the author of the book *Build to Last*, Jim Collins, has said, "Values are the roots from which an organisation continuously gets its supply as well as grounding — build on them!"

10

Three Aspects of Success

WHO DOESN'T WANT TO BE SUCCESSFUL? Forget the intensely competitive corporate world, today even children studying in schools and colleges crave success. So do folks in their own homes and societies.

Workshops and seminars are conducted on how to be successful. Entire organisations spend huge amounts of time, money, efforts and energy in becoming successful, and making their teams successful.

But what exactly is success? And how does one really become successful?

Well, success is a relative term.

The parameters for success change from person to person. However, when we study the lives of successful people, we come across some core values and actions on the basis of which they succeeded. Learning these core principles will help each one of us succeed too.

Even our own Indian hero Chanakya had delved deep into the subject of success.

He said:

"Success is threefold – that attainable by the power of counsel is success by counsel, that attainable by the power of might is success by might, that attainable by the power of energy is success by energy." (6.2.34)

Let us look at each of these separately:

- Success By Counsel

Every person needs an advisor. The better the advisor, the

better one is guaranteed to succeed. In fact, one should aim at having the best advisor all the time.

Chanakya, in another chapter of the *Arthashastra*, had said, "Any undertaking that one takes should be with the help of advisors who are specialists in that particular field."

If you ever have a choice between a mediocre teacher who charges less, and the best teacher who charges more, choose the second option.

You would, thus, minimise possible risks and also reach your goal faster.

- Success By Might

Muscle power is strength too. But might also means what benefits one derives due to one's position, or the chair that one holds.

A mighty person can take many quick decisions based on his authority and his execution capacity. Apart from holding such a high and responsible position, another way for becoming mighty is to associate with someone mightier than oneself.

- Success By Energy

This is called will-power. A person can achieve success on the basis of the enthusiasm and the passion he shows.

A highly inspired and energetic person is very contagious. Anyone who meets such a person also feels charged up. Great leaders had this power. They were those who could mesmerise masses with their oratory skills. Such energetic people can also make the most lethargic person productive.

This is akin to what Napoleon once said, "It requires a

stroke of genius to awaken the mass consciousness. In any given century, only a few can do that!"

11

Power Management

A SCHOLAR HAD ONCE DEFINED *Artha* as 'power' in the ancient Indian texts. This gives us a different, yet an apt meaning of the word *Arthashastra*. Thus, Chanakya's *Arthashastra* can be taken to be a book on 'power management'.

Such a book would be extremely useful for a person who holds a top leadership position and who should know which card to play at what time. Chanakya was a master in the field of power management and, throughout the *Arthashastra*, various options are given to the king.

In the seventh book of Kautilya's *Arthashastra*, Chanakya defines six situations and six different measures for handling them.

He says:

"These are really six measures, because of differences in the situations." (7.1.5)

Why does Chanakya promote alternative moves to deal with different situations?

The reason is simple — no two situations are the same and a unique 'strategy' must be applied for every situation.

If we understand just this, we will understand how to manage power. Let us take up some of the most common situations a corporate leader could come across:

- People Situations

As soon as a person attains power, the first thing he has to handle is the people working under him. In fact, the success of his career depends on not only how he will handle his own people, but also those who work for the competitor.

Each person is different, and it is important to understand how human beings act and react in different situations.

There have to be alternative strategies for every person and group. A study of human psychology will prove helpful in this very important task.

- Knowledge Situations

As the world moves towards a 'knowledge economy', the competitive advantage will be held by people who are ahead of others in the information sphere.

Today, companies are investing in research and development globally. You can either predict the future, or create it.

The future belongs to those who can not only think differently, but also create products and services that people will seek in the future.

- Material Situations

Here, material means money, machines, and even technology. The way business is done is changing drastically.

So what plans does a CEO have in place to handle rising costs, rapid technological changes and financial instability? A leader has to analyse each issue and create alternative and back-up plans.

There are always two routes — either let the situation come up first and then change accordingly. Or study and understand the situation even before it comes up to be ready with the right alternatives. In other words, being prepared for the inevitable change.

So, get into the habit of creating alternatives in every given situation. This is how one can manage power efficiently.

12

Bosses Are Answerable

ALL SALARIED PEOPLE HAVE, at some time or the other, given into wishful thinking — 'If I were the boss, I would have done this...' The general feeling is 'Had I been the boss myself, I wouldn't have to report to anyone. I would be the ultimate — no questions asked!'

This is simply not true. Every boss has a boss above him. Every leader is answerable to someone else. Well, who is this someone? If I am the chairman of a company, then there should be no one above me, right?... Wrong!

Chanakya had said:

"Only, the king, behaving in this manner (following the rules given to a king), obtains heaven, otherwise hell." (3.7.38)

According to him, every king is given a code of conduct (written or unwritten) and the duties and responsibilities that have to be borne.

If the king follows this code, he becomes a good leader

and need not fear hell. Basically, this refers to moral control. But who exactly bosses over our boss? Is he responsible to anyone? The answer is yes.

- To Stakeholders

Usually, it is understood that the person at the top is answerable to only those from whom he has taken money, like financiers and lenders. However, this is only partly true.

Modern management theories have evolved from being responsible not only to shareholders, but also to all 'stakeholders'. A stakeholder is not just one who controls shares, but also others like the employees, suppliers, and all partners in the business.

- To Government and Society

Every company is governed by certain laws. It can be the law of that particular nation, defined by the government through corporate and company laws. It can also be laws of industry associations that establish common standards which all members are supposed to follow.

But, most importantly, each company is also responsible to the society of which it is a part. Today, Corporate Social Responsibility (CSR) is a driving force in many businesses. Every company has to be socially responsible.

- To Self

Well, one may not follow others. One may not even like government policies, the industry standards or existing social rules. But the one person that you cannot run away from is 'yourself'.

You are still answerable to your parents and your teachers. More than anyone else, a leader is supposed to be reporting to himself. So ask yourself these questions and take stock — "Have I done my duty well?", "Am I following what I am supposed to do?"

After all, at the end of the journey, you and only you are left alone. And, as all religions and scriptures say, "Finally, it is between you and God."

13

Applying *Arthashastra* in Business

WHENEVER I OFFER TRAINING sessions on *Arthashastra*, the first question I hear people ask is, 'Chanakya and *Arthashastra* existed in the past, but what does *Arthashastra* have for me?', 'What are the benefits I will get by studying this?'

Well, as Chanakya himself said about the benefits:

"This science (of Arthashastra) brings into being and preserves spiritual good, material well-being and pleasures, and destroys spiritual evil, material loss, and hatred." (15.1.72)

- Protecting and Expanding

If one has achieved something, it has to be protected. If you earn a few lakh rupees, it has to be saved and protected. You should not let anyone steal it. At the same time, we should think of how to expand these lakhs into crores. This is where 'investment planning' comes in.

Similarly, studying the science of *Arthashastra* helps one accomplish as well as preserve spiritual good, i.e. the goodwill and ethics that one has cultivated, along with material benefits (financial and lifestyle).

In addition to achieving, *Arthashastra* even gives us strategies on how to expand and improve on these.

- Destroy the Wrong

Only protecting and expanding the good is not enough. One has to destroy the evils also. This is a two-way street. *Arthashastra* destroys spiritual evils like laziness and lethargy.

It also helps in destroying material and monetary losses with the help of good planning and implementation. Best of all, *Arthashastra* helps in destroying even hatred. You see, hatred is a negative emotion that is self-destructive.

As the saying goes, "A man who is angry destroys himself first." Even in a war, one should respect the enemy and not fight because of hatred alone.

- Expansion of Knowledge

By studying the *Arthashastra*, one increases knowledge and experience. How, you ask? Chanakya's treatise may be theoretical, but studying it automatically translates into practical application in daily business life — the best way to gain wisdom.

But its most important lesson is that one learns by teaching, i.e. sharing wisdom with others. So do not forget to do this as it will help and support your peers just as it did for you.

14

Inherited Company

There are first-generation entrepreneurs, and then there are the 'businessmen' who have inherited their parents' creations. What matters in both these cases is how the person manages the business.

While most of the work has already been done by the parents, Chanakya still had advice for children born with a silver spoon in their mouth:

"In the case of inherited territory, he should cover up the father's defects and display his virtues." (13.5.23)

All establishments, inevitably, have their negative points along with various positive aspects. Chanakya advised those benefiting from an inheritance to look at the positives of the business and change the negative points with their own positives.

- Identify the Positive Aspects

As far as inheriting a business is concerned, we find that the previous generation did the worst work — starting up, sales, capturing the market, etc. They went through some real hard times when there was no capital, uneven cash flows, when even such basic necessities like infrastructure and other comforts were not available.

At the end of the tunnel, they saw the light, and eventually started making money. But, more than the money, it's their original experience that makes the most valuable inheritance. This knowledge will prevent people from repeating mistakes.

- Neutralise the Negatives

Earlier generations lived in different times. The market conditions were different then. Economic conditions were different. Even government policies and structures were unique then.

Everything, right from technology to travel, and even communications, was slow. However, we should study these situations as next-generation leaders striving to fill top positions. Only then we will be able to see the business from a new perspective.

- Be a 'Positive' Change

After getting the power to make decisions, move your company slowly to the next level without giving any serious jerks to the existing system. In other words, install the required new systems and processes, but do so while maintaining relations with your previous clients, and employees while growing your business too.

Basically, you should come across as a new-age leader who is also grounded in the traditional values on the basis of which your seniors built the business.

And when you finally commence operations in your new capacity, remember this — "What I have, is my father's gift to me. What I do with what I have, is my gift to my father."

15

A Public Awakening

HISTORY HAS TIME AND AGAIN proved that people and their opinions cannot be suppressed for too long. The oppressed people may not openly revolt against their rulers, but only till a particular point. After that the frustrations will build up and a revolution will break out.

Even in the modern day democracy we find that public awakening is dangerous for the government. Once the public loses its patience and takes to the streets, even the most powerful rulers will crumble. After such demonstrations, several tainted ministers have had to resign.

Chanakya had clearly pointed out how to avoid such a situation:

"In the happiness of the subjects, lies the benefit of the king, and in what is beneficial for the subjects, is his own benefit." (1.19.34)

If a leader is not able to keep his people happy, and instead thinks of his own benefit all the time, he will definitely end up being dethroned. Just look at the way the top politicians have had to bow to the popular opinion of the citizens and give up their positions.

It's a 'perform or get out' environment. Gone are those days when people could take things for granted. One has to be at their best and deliver results. If not, the people's wrath will be awakened.

- For Politicians

According to me, politicians need to get one thing straight

— from now onwards, you cannot continue to operate in a loose manner. You need to learn better management skills.

And to all those politicians who are reading this, in case you still don't know about political management, learn from the *Arthashastra* about how a state must be governed.

- **For Citizens**

Be an enlightened citizen of the nation. If you have a problem and you can see that things are not getting done, make sure you do your bit. The fuel for any revolution is continuity. Follow up till you get results. Make use of the power of democracy and of your precious vote.

There are two things every citizen has — duties and rights. Fulfill your duties as a citizen first, then demand your rights and, more importantly, ensure that you get them.

- **For Youngsters**

I was in Pune and Nashik, conducting leadership training programmes. To my pleasant surprise, I found more and more youngsters attending these sessions. One of them asked me, "Sir, why not start a new political party?"

I replied, "Good idea my boy, but convert your idea into action." It was not a mini-sermon. Rather, it was my belief in the potential of a youngster to channelise his energy positively.

As Swami Chinmayananda said, "The youth are not useless — they are used less. The youth are not careless — they are cared for less."

Qualities of a Leader

16

Total Alertness

THE CENTRAL VIGILANCE COMMISSION OF INDIA has declared that various government organisations and Public Sector Units must observe a 'Vigilance Awareness Week', every year. This week coincides with the birthday of Sardar Vallabhai Patel — the Iron Man of India.

Sardar Patel had a very important role to play in the building of modern India by overpowering the princely states and uniting them successfully under a central governance. This had been done by Kautilya in the 4th Century B.C as well. He had united the various kingdoms under a central governance led by his student, Chandragupta Maurya.

Kautilya was the first person to have systematically given 'vigilance' a very important dimension in a state organisation's management structure.

The Oxford English Dictionary defines *vigilance* as, 'keeping careful watch for possible danger or difficulties'. From a corporate standpoint it gives us two perspectives from which to view the same subject. One must protect oneself from external threats as well as from internal mismanagement.

At the external level, an organisation has to be alert about such dangers as competition and takeovers. For this, it needs to have a very powerful intelligence network. In most companies today, market intelligence is a very important activity. There is special technology for getting valuable information.

However, being vigilant 'internally' is more important and very difficult. The problems within an organisation are much more difficult to manage, as we deal with our own people. An army commander may be able to fight and withdraw the enemy troops at the borders, but may not be able to handle a revolt by his own young son.

Important information about accounts, customer databases, and management strategies are very critical to an organisation. These need to be protected from being leaked.

How does one do this? *Arthashastra* guides us about handling these problems. Kautilya says,

"He (leader) should constantly hold an inspection of their works, men being inconstant in their minds." (2.9.3)

It is the primary responsibility of the leader to continuously check all important data as well as the activities in one's organisation. The leader has to be very alert about the movements of his employees.

He has to give the employees targets and deadlines to keep them focused on their work. Secondly, he has to continuously monitor their work.

Why is it so? Because the human mind is very fickle. Employees have a tendency to slip into laziness if deadlines and targets are not set. There is also a possibility of one getting influenced by corruption if the fear of punishments is not strong enough.

As Akio Morita, the founder of Sony Corporation said, "I am dealing not just with my employees but with the *minds* of my employees." Therefore it is important to understand the employees at the level of their minds, to prevent corruption as well as to ensure productivity from each of them.

Thus, vigilance is 'total alertness' on both fronts — internal and external.

17

Advice to Entrepreneurs

STARTING YOUR OWN BUSINESS and running it is no easy task, especially when you have no previous business experience. But that is how entrepreneurs are born. They start with an 'idea' and a dream to succeed. Most of them do not know the path they need to take, but the confidence they have takes them through all the ups and downs till the final destination where their idea is finally converted to financial success.

The most critical period in an entrepreneur's life is when he has already experimented with his idea a little, and struggled the most, but money has not yet filled his pockets. Now, he sits down and wonders what went wrong. All his near and dear ones are taking the opportunity to prove that he was wrong to have taken this path.

Hold on, says Kautilya, do not get into a mental trap at this stage:

"Wealth will slip away from the foolish person, who continuously consults the stars; for wealth is the star of wealth; what will the stars

do? Capable men will certainly secure wealth at least after a hundred trials." (9.4.26)

Your final *big* financial leap in business may be just round the corner. But getting frustrated after such a long period of failure, it is natural for one to wonder if fate and luck has really been on one's side.

That is when we turn to fortune tellers, astrologers, and palm readers. You start to consult the zodiac, the sun, and star signs. But remember, your constant efforts are the only way out. Do not consult the stars. What will those innocent looking balls of burning gas, which appear as glowing points in the night sky, do? Wealth alone is the star of wealth. You have already put in a lot of efforts, time and money into the 'idea' you truly believe in. Just continue doing this.

Capable men will finally convert the whole idea into an 'amazing balance sheet'. The final leap may come in any manner — a big order, a turnaround client or a big investor. But one needs to keep undergoing these trials — a hundred times.

This is the path followed by Bill Gates. Who thought he would become the richest man in the world in such a short time? This is the route taken by Narayan Murthy, or any other victorious entrepreneur, before they touched the success called 'wealth'.

Madam C.J. Walker, creator of a popular line of African-American hair care products and America's first black female millionaire said, "I had to make my own living and my own opportunity! But I made it! Don't sit down and wait for the opportunities to come. Get up and make them!"

18

Multiple Tasking

THE SUCCESS STORIES OF GREAT organisations start with the dream and will of one single person. Once the dream starts becoming a reality the little stream becomes a massive flow.

As the organisation grows, work also grows and more and more people join in. From a one-man army, it becomes a full-fledged army with its own dedicated lieutenants and soldiers. Finally, all the teamwork helps the organisation reach the summit of success.

Hence the key to success for a leader lies in effective delegation.

Why is delegation required? Kautilya says,

"Because of the simultaneity of undertakings, their manifoldness and their having to be carried out in many different places, he (leader) should cause them to be carried by ministers, unperceived (by him), so that there is no loss of place and time." (1.9.8)

Delegation is required due to the following reasons:

- Work Happens Simultaneously

In an office, various departments work simultaneously at the same time. Each of them is specialised in a particular area. Sales, accounts, marketing, HR, R&D, and many other processes go on continuously.

- Work Happens at Various Places

These multiple tasks are carried out not only by various people, but at various places. Some of the work happens inside the office, while many other tasks are carried out outside the office. In a big organisation, work happens in various branches, and also in various countries.

Decision-making should be decentralised and given to various managers. The benefit is the saving of time and place. As they say, "In business — time is money." Delayed decisions lead to loss of time and opportunities.

A few tips for effective delegation are:

- Selection

Good decision makers should be made managers and department heads. An effective manager does not get stuck while taking decisions. He may make mistakes but after correcting himself, the work goes on at the right speed.

- Setting Up the MIS

The head of the organisation needs to set up a good reporting system. In corporate language this is technically called the Management Information System (MIS). Many software tools are available for this, or an organisation can create one for its own use.

- Training

The decision makers have to be trained to report all activities by using the MIS. This training ensures that everyone in the organisation can effectively use the reports. With the internet revolution, one can access these reports anytime and anywhere. It is also cost effective.

- Control

The leader can keep track of the various developments and the shortcomings in each area on a daily basis. He can control the whole organisation with the help of a well-planned system.

Peter Drucker, the father of modern management once said, "Initially delegation is not easy. It gives a feeling of insecurity. However, one realises that it leads to freedom."

19

Open-Door Policy

THE LEADER OF AN ORGANISATION has to be very alert and vigilant. He has to be aware that he might receive wrong as well as manipulated information from various sources. He has to be most wary about his own 'middle-men'.

Middle-men for the senior management would be the junior managers and those who deal with the lower staff on a daily basis. These middle-men report to the seniors all that happens at the lower end.

However, being totally dependent on the middle-men can be dangerous. If one gets too dependent they can change reports, encourage corruption, and also leak important data.

Therefore, Kautilya advises an open-door policy right not only for those at the junior-most level in the organisation, but also those in the senior management.

"He (leader) should allow unrestricted entrance to those wishing to see him in connection with their affairs." (1.19.26)

Any person who wants to communicate with the seniors

about their affairs should be encouraged as it helps bridge the gap of communication.

Unrestricted entrance means middle-men cannot restrict, or control whom you meet and share information with. In various organisations one has to pass through secretaries to get the work done. Secretaries are required to leverage your work. But the moment one becomes dependent on them and they start taking decisions concerning 'people' for you — watch out!

A few benefits of an open-door policy are:

- Direct Information

Many officials, especially from sales and marketing directly deal in the market as well as with the outside world. They are the eyes and ears of the company. The senior management can keep a finger on the pulse of the market and competition by communicating with them directly.

- Avoiding External Threats

When employees are assured that they are 'listened' to, they will not feel the need for external supporting agencies such as labour unions and political parties. Most of the external threats to organisations stem from 'internal' insecurities felt by their own people.

- Faster Decisions

Important decisions do not get delayed when problems are fixed as they occur. Decisions taken at the right time avoid confusion and misunderstandings.

- Emotional Bonding

Subordinates begin to feel a deep emotional bond with the leader who makes it clear, usually by example, that he will be by their side in tight situations as well as when there are joys to share. The presence of such a leader builds a sense of security and faith in the team.

One of the basic human requirements is to have someone who can 'listen' to your problems. Effective leaders understand this psychological need. Therefore, successful leaders always communicate to their team, "Okay, I will be there whenever you have a problem."

20

Ethics in Business

THERE IS A HUGE MISUNDERSTANDING about Kautilya, also known as Chanakya. People generally believe that he was a shrewd and cunning person. That's just a myth.

While training his students in the management of a kingdom, he emphasised the importance of having a sound philosophy in order to become a good leader. Ethics and morals were top priority for him. In the very first chapter of *Arthashastra*, titled *The Topic of Training*, he outlines the importance of a spiritual foundation.

Therefore he says in the *Arthashastra*,

"Philosophy is ever thought of as the lamp of all sciences, as the means of all actions (and) as the support of all laws (and duties)." (1.3.12)

The root of any business lies in its core value system — its philosophy. This was also pointed out by the father of modern management, Peter Drucker. He said, "Profits are by-products of business, not its very goal." In the above verse, Kautilya brings out the finer points of the importance of ethics in business.

- Guidance

The value system created by the founders of an organisation always becomes the guiding force for the organisation. Even during calamities and difficult times, these values become a lighthouse, providing direction. Like a lamp, it guides us through darkness.

- Decision in Action

How to proceed, even when drawing up a plan, is always the big question in business. Either one can take the easy route where success is quick and, yet, short-lived. Or, one can take the road less travelled where success is delayed, but is everlasting. Only an ethical person can easily handle these tough decisions.

- Adhering to Law

A good businessman is not just law-fearing, but also law-abiding. He follows the law of the land as set up by the constitution. At the same time, he also understands the higher universal law of nature. His thoughts become very powerful. Such a businessman contributes to society and brings great economic prosperity to all persons connected with him.

- Doing One's Duty

For such a person, duty is a priority over rights. He understands the importance of giving more than what is taken and producing more than what is consumed. His work and duty is not influenced by pressure, but is born out of joy and service.

Once, an Indian company which believes in ethically conducting business was asked by a politician for a small bribe to clear a huge project. The sum was small compared to the size of the project. However, the philosophy of the organisation did not support bribing. The result? They dropped the project. The gain — it still continues to be the most trusted company in the country.

Kautilya would have called such a highly spiritual leader and businessman 'Rajarishi'.

21

Start Now

THE INDIAN ECONOMY IS currently functioning at its best. Foreign investors are pouring money into India. Job opportunities have opened up. Starting a new business is no more limited to the rich class.

In today's corporate scenario, there are multiple opportunities for anything you want to do. Yet, we find people sad, stressed, and worrying about the future.

Kautilya suggests,

"Having found a matter for consideration, he should not allow time to pass." (1.15.45)

Do not wait for any 'golden' moment to start what you always wanted to do. The best time is not the *muhurat* the pundit suggests, nor even the 'right dates' that come up in a calendar. It is right here and now!

After having considered a matter, start work on it

immediately. Remember always that the journey of a thousand miles begins with the first step.

While starting any project or assignment, a few tips from the *Arthashastra* would be helpful:

- Self-Effort

There is always a problem when it comes to starting anything. Maximum energy is required at this point. You need to challenge yourself to shake off your laziness. Do not procrastinate. A job started is a job half-done. Just start!

- Prepare a Plan

Starting does not mean just getting excited. You need to have a direction for how you are going to reach your goal. Take a piece of paper (or open a new file in your computer) and jot down the points. Give shape to your thoughts. Prepare a blueprint of what you want to do. Begin with the end in the mind.

- Consult an Expert

If you are not sure if your ideas are practical, ask an expert for advice. Take the help of someone who can guide you to make your dream a reality. It very important not to go to people who say, "It will not work." In the initial stages, such negative energy must be avoided. You will kill the child even before it is born. Your consultant should display a positive attitude and should be successful in his own field.

- Work Out Your Plan

All said and done, you have to work out your plan. Do not spend too much time trying to make your plan perfect. Plans are theories that can be successful only if they are given the wings of practical application. Once you start, the help, and required resources will come your way. You will learn a lot as you keep putting more and more efforts into your dream. You can keep improving your plan along the way.

However, it is important to complete what you have started to achieve. It is not important how many new things you have started. What is important is how many of them you have completed. Complete what you have started. And, then, start again after you have completed!

22

Knowledge for a Leader

SWAMI VIVEKANANDA HAD ONCE predicted that India would rise on the basis of its knowledge. True enough, knowledge has become the greatest asset of our country. As more and more projects are being outsourced to India, we have to focus more on the strength of our knowledge.

Whether it is KPO (Knowledge Process Outsourcing) or R&D (Research and Development), India has great advantages over its counterparts.

However, this knowledge cannot be restricted to just hiring intelligent managers from the top B-schools. The leader or the Chief Executive Officer (CEO) of the organisation himself should be a knowledge seeker.

Kautilya advises,

"Just as an elephant, blinded by intoxication and mounted by an intoxicated driver, crushes whatever it finds (on the way), so the king, not possessed of the eye of science, and (hence) blind, has risen to destroy the citizens and the country people." (1.14.7)

The CEO of an organisation holds a position of power and is the commander and the decision-maker. However, if he gets intoxicated by his power and position alone, it will definitely not be long before he loses his chair, and may even destroy the organisation itself.

This is where we need Kautilya's advice about focusing on knowledge. A leader should focus on making his organisation a knowledge organisation. But, first he has to start with himself.

The *Arthashastra* offers some advice on this:

- Gather More Information

A CEO should have his information-gathering systems in place. He should get any information he requires at the speed of thought. He can use technology to gather information quickly. But always remember — information does not mean knowledge.

- Study the Information Acquired

It's very important for a leader to study and analyse the information he gathers. He should spend at least an hour per day reading books and learning something new. He must meet experts from different fields, at least once a week.

- Experiment

What the CEO has learnt should be applied in the organisation. Try a new method, invest in a new technology. Take measures. Calculate risks. A part of the

budget should be allocated for research and development.
- Train

Next, he should train his own staff and team members about the new knowledge. No leader should be afraid that he will lose his position and authority if his subordinates become better than him. That only shows insecurity and ego. Learn to delegate and trust your subordinates.

Today, we require more and more knowledge-oriented CEOs. As Rabindranath Tagore wrote in the *Gitanjali*,

"Where the mind is without fear and the head is held high,

... where knowledge is free... ,

....Into that heaven of freedom my father let my country awake..."

23

Decisionmaking

TO BECOME A LEADER YOU should *think* like a leader. Sit down and observe what qualities good leaders have. And then start practising them. One of the important qualities of a leader is good decisionmaking.

Chanakya says,

"He should hear (at once) every urgent matter, (and) not put it off. An (affair) postponed becomes difficult to settle or even impossible to settle." (1.19.30)

There is a lot of work that cannot move forward without the leader's final sanction. Thus, Chanakya suggests that if a subordinate comes to him with an urgent matter, he should listen to him at once. If he postpones a decision, the pressure gets piled up and then the situation gets out of control.

A leader has to be a fast thinker, a fast decisionmaker, and a fast implementer. He has no time to waste. Analysing is good, but moving ahead is more important.

How can one become a good decision maker?

- Do Not Be Afraid to Make Mistakes

In an interview, a CEO was asked the secret of his success. "It is by taking timely decisions," he replied. "How do you know if your decisions are correct?" he was asked. The CEO snapped, "By taking wrong decisions."

Every child has to fall before he learns to walk and run. Do not be afraid of making mistakes. But what is important is to learn from these mistakes. At the same time, do not keep making mistakes eternally.

- Set Up a Time Frame

While you are planning and thinking about an assignment or project, give yourself enough time to think about various possibilities. But there must be a time frame by when you will have to take some action. Only then will theory meet practice.

- Encourage Others to Take Decisions

Work gets stuck when it is dependent on a single person. Learn to delegate smaller decisions to your subordinates. Your organisation should become a self-managed mechanism. Train others and make them responsible. You should only be dealing with the important matters at the top.

The game should be bigger than the player. The

organisation should be bigger than the employees. The purpose should be bigger than you and me.

24

The Spiritual Side

THE HEAD, OR THE BOSS, in any organisation has an additional responsibility these days — being an important contributor to society.

After all, modern businessmen provide employment, create revenue for the government, and are socially-contributing entities. If the head of an organisation works with the right attitude, the king (leader) not only experiences its benefits in this world, but also in the next world.

Chanakya says,

"Carrying out his own duty, the king, who protects the subjects according to law, leads to heaven; one who does not protect or who inflicts an unjust punishment, his condition would be the reverse of this." (3.1.41)

Now, please remember that Chanakya did not literally mean 'heaven' or 'hell'. Both are states of mind. When you are happy and satisfied, that mental state is heaven. While, stress, tension, uncertainty is hell for any human being.

So how can we transform our work place into heaven?

- Carry Out Your Own Work Well

The prime duty of a leader is to protect and take care of his subordinates. Instead of thinking about 'my gain', he has to think about 'our gain'. This is an attitude that no business school can teach. It comes with a sense of responsibility and commitment. Great leaders have strong shoulders and a big heart. As you practise this, you will realise the depth of the age-old adage — work is worship.

- Respect the Laws of the Land

In the course of your duty, abide by the law. The law of the government and its policies have to be carried out properly. No illegal work can give any person satisfaction. It only makes you insecure. Remember, many organisations have ruined themselves by getting into illegitimate work. Pay your taxes, and be a company that also plays a role in social development. Also, understand the laws of nature. Enjoy life but never over-indulge in anything. A sense of balance needs to be maintained.

- Be Just

As a leader, you are a law unto yourself. If there is a conflict, your subjects (employees) will come to you seeking justice. At such times, your integrity can help resolve issues in the just and right manner. Chanakya said in the *Arthashastra*, "A king who is severe in punishment becomes a terror. The one who is too mild is taken for granted. However, the king just with rod is honoured and respected."

This art has to be developed.

In the olden days, the king was considered to be God. In fact, there is an Indian saying — *Raja Pratyaksha Devata,* meaning a good king is God himself. Hence, all business leaders can create heaven, or hell, in their companies all by themselves!

25

An Eye for Detail

UNDERSTANDING THE GROWTH of any business entity is a beautiful study in itself. Most corporates usually started with one man's dream. Then, a like-minded person decided to become a partner, and provide support.

The next step involves a group of people joining the vision and, finally, the firm gradually expands into a large corporation.

When a company keeps growing in terms of sales and revenues, the number of transactions it does also grows. Now, that's something that the leaders and founders may not have the time to keep an eye on, as they have to focus on the larger picture.

At such times, we require supervisors from different departments to look into the details of all transactions and activities.

The advice given by Chanakya to the commodity stores supervisor gives us an insight into how important micro-management is for large corporations.

Chanakya says,

"He should personally observe the amount of increase or decrease in the grains when pounded, ground, or fried, and when they are moistened, dried, or cooked." (2.15.24)

So for every small task, there should be systems in place to monitor and supervise it. And, since these systems alone cannot be helpful, the department incharge should also 'personally' observe the details.

Now how can the Head of a Department (HoD) do this? Here are some tips:

- Create a System

Firstly, create a system to regularly record transactions. The first step in creating a system is to list down what is necessary to know. Do not try to make a perfect system on the first day itself. Take one step at a time. Your system could be just a notebook, or a simple Excel file. As your requirement grows, you can invest in better software programs, or even an ERP program. But first, start from where you are.

- Daily Monitoring

Creating systems isn't enough. You have to also control the systems. No system is complete without a person monitoring it from the top. Therefore, the next step is to arrange for daily and regular supervision. In the initial stages, you will have to give more of your time to understand whether your methods work. Then, as you get a grip over the methods, monitor them from time to time.

- Conduct Surprise Checks

This is the best way to keep people on their toes, and has remained so for years. This method is not only for companies, but also for schools, homes, and all those places where you have to lead a group of people.

Always remember that you should never leave the game till you win it completely. So, define your parameters for achieving victory. The best way to be in the game is to keep raising the bar every time you reach it.

26

Being Energetic

BEFORE YOU START ON ANY task, the first requirement is you should be optimistic. If you mix this attitude with the right amount of dynamism and energy, you're set for success.

Why else do you think all the 'motivational speakers' are so well-received globally? It's their workshops that transform a person who is feeling low into an enthusiastic contributor to society.

Chanakya outlines similar qualities in the *Arthashastra* as well:

"Bravery, resentment, quickness, and dexterity — these are the qualities of energy." (6.1.5)

In one line, Chanakya tells us how, in addition to enthusiasm, energy is important too. He has gone into great detail to make us understand what energy means in the above verse.

These points are also leadership qualities that should be developed by any person who aspires to be successful not only in the corporate world, but also in life:

- Bravery

Literally speaking, bravery means 'facing something frightening, or unpleasant in a courageous way'. A brave person is ready to face life's unpleasant events with a strong heart and tremendous will-power to carry on.

He is ready to fight and win challenges enroute his goal. This is also the most important quality of a Kshatriya —

the warrior described by all Indian scriptures as well as the *Arthashastra*.

- Resentment

Resentment means anger, hatred, and yes, even bitterness. Now this may sound negative. However, understand that being a little unsatisfied with our current status can push us towards achieving the bigger things in life.

So, be angry with yourself for thinking small. Hate the low mental and vulgar values that we entertain. Be bitter about the comfort zone we get into.

Push yourself to the next level. This 'positive' negativity adds spice to life.

- Quickness

Time is an important ingredient for success. A person who aspires to be successful needs to be quick and fast while taking decisions.

When a leader was once asked how to develop the skill of quick decisionmaking, he answered, "Be around people who are not afraid of making mistakes." So, move on in life as quickly as you can.

- Dexterity

Here, it means the ability to adapt and continue. It's best defined by the famous saying — When the going gets tough, the tough gets going. We all start on a journey, but only a few adapt to the changes and overcome problems.

Swami Chinmayananda said, "There are three kinds of people — first, those who do not start work because of the fear of obstacles. Second, those who start, but stop when they face obstacles. And, third, those who work inspite of obstacles and overcome it!"

Now, you decide which kind of person you are.

27

Improve What You Inherit

AN ENTREPRENEUR WAS ONCE told by his mentor, "When you start a business, you will have to struggle a lot. The success you finally get will be enjoyed by your children, not you!"

Every generation benefits from the struggle of its predecessors. However, thanks to the human mindset, we always tend to look for what was built incorrectly, rather than what was built right.

This is where Chanakya comes in:

"In the case of inherited territory, he should cover up the father's defects and display his virtues." (13.5.23)

Even Swami Chinmayananda had similar advice — every generation has got two responsibilities: to correct the mistakes of the past, and to create something for the future. But how do we apply this in our careers and family lives?

- Look at the Positive Side

When we inherit something, like a car, we immediately think, 'Oh, what an old car. I wish I could get a new one.' But train your mind to look at the positive side. "So what? It's better than having no car."

Similarly, when you get an old computer to use as soon as you join a new office, be thankful that at least there is a computer for you to start working on. These steps will tune your mind to look at the bright side of what our elders provided, without any effort.

- Understand What is Missing

With their limited vision or resources, our elders gave you whatever you now have. Surely they must have wanted to give us something better, but their conditions must have been different. They missed the luxury that our generation can access with ease.

If, by chance, our seniors did a mistake due to short-sightedness, try to understand the reason. Instead of condemning them, 'empathise'. Put yourself in their shoes.

Even in your company, you should study what is missing instead of blaming the management. Try to 'understand' the reason behind present circumstances and then try to improve the situation.

- Create Something New

Be the change you are seeking. If something is not available, create it yourself. Put in some efforts and do the needful yourself.

If you find that systems in your firm are not updated, study the technology yourself and apply them. Basically, you should convert your tendency to blame others, into a tendency to be thankful.

A young boy once told his father, "Your generation doesn't understand anything. You did not have mobiles, computers or the Internet."

The dad replied, "Yes, it's true. So our generation created the mobiles and computers for you to use. Now let's see what you will create for your children!"

28

Setting an Example

BEING AN EXPERT IN POLITICAL science and even statesmanship, Chanakya emphasised the importance of discipline in a governance system. However, he also knew that the ministers and bureaucrats would have to follow the rules themselves.

Therefore, Chanakya had said:

"The administrator and the magistrates should first keep in check the heads of departments and their subordinates." (Book 2 & 3)

Let us see why this is necessary and how it applies to our offices and organisations:

- Discipline Starts From the Top

If you are the boss, you are the sole rule-maker. But then you should be the first follower of any rule. One cannot create policies and just insist that others follow it. Discipline starts with you. When you become self-disciplined, others tend to fall in line automatically.

- Leaders Are Followed

A leader's position is very critical and sensitive. Your subordinates do not just do what you say — they follow your every action! You are always observed minutely by people around you.

If the leader is highly enthusiastic, the subordinates will also be enthusiastic. If the leader is lazy and slack while performing his duties, so will his subordinates.

The same thought had been brought out in the *Gita* when Lord Krishna said, "Whatever standard the leader sets, others follow." So set high standards, and make sure you follow them yourself.

- An 'Unforgivable' Mistake

Always remember one thing — small mistakes are not small if committed by people at the top. That's because such actions impact the entire organisation.

Chanakya went to the extent of saying that if a common man commits a mistake, the punishment is one unit (like one year). But if the same mistake is committed by the leader, the punishment is four units.

This is because if the leader makes a mistake, it is akin to the entire group making a mistake. Hence, a leader should think twice before taking any decision.

A leader with a vision is the prime requirement of any good company, organisation, or society. The next step is to transform his visions into reality.

This happens through hard work and the ability to inspire others to pitch in and dedicate themselves to the eventual goal. And all this is possible with self-discipline.

29

Work Through Problems

SWAMI CHINMAYANANDAJI HAD once said, "In any work, problems are unavoidable. It only ends when we are in the grave."

Thus, life can be said to be a continuing series of problems. But, you should remember that people become successful when they learn to handle these problems, instead of allowing it to overpower them.

It helps to know how problems are created. Chanakya offers some important information:

"Internal (hindrance) is hindrance by the chiefs, external is the hindrance caused by enemies or forest-tribes." (8.4.48)

All of us must have experienced such 'hindrances', especially when we want to start something new. We should understand how these hindrances begin and how to avoid them. Chanakya said there are three kinds of problem creators:

- The Chief

Quite often, the boss himself becomes a problem-creator. One experience of this is enough to make us hate our bosses, especially when they reject what we think is a good idea. But don't be discouraged.

Enquire about the reason for the rejection and see if they are justified. If you are the boss yourself, then become an ideal leader by developing leadership qualities and understanding your workers.

- The Enemies

The enemies are our competitors. When we have a plan to execute, they almost immediately have a counter plan. This is apparent in the advertising industry which goes to great extremes to prove that one's own client has a product that is much better than that of the competitor.

But remember to respect your enemies as well. Even when at war, your actions should not be driven out of hatred or anger. This is because the best warfare strategies are devised by those who remain calm.

- **The Forest-Tribes**

A firm normally encounters opposition from local groups when entering a new territory or market (forest-tribes in the time of kings). Always remember that this particular opposition arises even if you are doing something for the greater good. The insecurities of the people who already live there will create problems for you. So, the first step is to win their confidence and ensure that it's a win-win situation for all.

30

Respect and Protect Women

BHISHMA, THE WARRIOR HERO in *Mahabharata*, had once advised Yudhishtira — "A society that does not respect women will perish." It was this lack of respect towards the fairer sex that caused the two great wars in our Hindu epics — the 18-day battle in *Mahabharata* after Draupadi was humiliated in front of all the men and in *Ramayana*, the war in Lanka when Sita was kidnapped by Ravana.

Even Chanakya refers to the priority that must be given to women during a crisis:

"From a dangerous situation he should move away with effort, after removing the women-folk." (7.5.46)

In other words, even when one has to run away from disaster, or a dangerous situation, he should do so only after rescuing the women. One may ask, where is the need for such lessons when there's so much gender equality?

Well, ask your own female friends and relatives whether they feel equal in society, and if any harassment aimed at their gender has ended completely.

Base your own decision on their answer. And if you believe a change in mindsets is a must, read on to see how we can respect and protect women in our daily lives:

- In Our Work Places

Today, the number of working women has increased in all areas. Be it in the field of business, education, or civil services.

All of us have to interact with women. Remember that men and women think differently. It's a basic psychological difference.

When men and women work on a common project together, they bring in different perspectives. Now if you are the boss, see to it that there is a gender mix in every project. If you are an employee, inculcate not only respect towards women, but also a receptiveness to their point of view.

- In Our Homes

While a house is incomplete without a woman, the women in our family also have talents that need to be given wings.

Identify their talents and give them freedom to explore their potential, regardless of whether it's your daughter, wife, sister, or mother.

- As a Nation

Even though women have proved themselves in every field, we still have a long way to go. Just look at the number of female infanticides we still hear about, the low percentage of girl literacy, the prevailing evil practice of dowry, etc.

No social work can be complete till women are empowered. We refer to our country as 'Mother India', but hardly allow her to have any daughters.

Swami Vivekananda had rightly said — "Educate the girl child and the nation will awaken."

31

Don't Forget Your People

FREEDOM FIGHTERS AND soldiers fight to protect their countries. But when we finally become victorious, it's our duty and responsibility to free the Prisoners of War (PoW) who have been captured by the opponents.

Chanakya had said the same thing:

"When grown in strength, he should bring about the liberation of the hostage." (7.17.32)

In the case of the Indian freedom struggle too, several members of the Indian National Army (INA) were held in prisons in the Andaman Islands. When we achieved freedom, they were rescued and also given awards and other national benefits.

It was the right thing to do, especially after the country had become victorious in her struggle for freedom. Now, how do we practise this in our organisations?

- Know Each Person and Group

The head of each organisation should be aware of those who fight for him. Keep track of the people who have been with you through difficult times. Spend some time with them and their families too.

You will be surprised to know of the sacrifices your employees and their families have to make sometimes. In the case of a large company, or nation, the leader should keep track of groups of people who have fought for him or her — communities, local committees, religious leaders, etc.

- Freedom is a Responsibility

After achieving the target, leaders should not think only about enjoying the resultant power. Instead, they must immediately meet with the people who fought for them. In companies too, when we have gone through a difficult phase — like a financial setback or a recession period — meet with those who have stayed committed and loyal.

So when you rise in life, understand that this freedom brings new responsibilities. Also, if someone is held hostage (or down with problems), immediately release them (solve their problems).

- Stories to Tell

Finally, never forget the most important task — making sure that the sacrifices made by your followers do not go unnoticed. Bring the heroes into the limelight and let them tell their stories. Document their struggle and let others get inspired.

These heroes are the pillars of any institution and should be rewarded. If any generation has to look back and it does not find any inspiring martyrs, they will take your hard-earned success for granted.

So, ensure people know what it took to reach where you are now. And the best way to do this is to recognise those who helped you become victorious.

32

Passing the Mantle

I WAS ONCE CONDUCTING a session for management students who were specialising in family-managed businesses. The students were second-or third-generation businessmen who hoped the course would help them take the businesses, started by their parents and grandparents, to the next level.

This reminded me of a verse from the *Arthashastra*:

"The kingdom continues in the succession of his sons and grandsons, free from dangers caused by men." (5.1.56)

One of the basic aims of Chanakya was that every kingdom should continue from one generation to the other, free from any danger. For this, he stressed the importance of good planning and training to make the inheritance of a kingdom fool-proof.

One extremely huge advantage of such an inheritance system is that the king gets to pass on the mantle on his own terms — choosing to make his exit, before being booted out!

Now, how do modern businessmen apply this thought to their own legacies?

- Train Your Children

The first and foremost task for any organisation's founder is to acquaint the next-generation with the firm's systems. There is simply no alternative to training your children in your own business. But, at times, it does not work well because the father may have very high expectations from his own children in business. And children may take a lot of their parents' good advice for granted and ignore them.

One solution adopted by many communities is to impart the requisite training to the children under the watchful eye of the founder's brother. Thus, the child gets trained while the family retains control over the business.

- Emphasis on Education

It's a fact that each generation has more opportunities for better education than the previous generation. So, seniors should capitalise on this and make it a point to educate their children by enrolling them in the best courses available. Education, even in business, should never be treated as an expense, but an investment which will have very high returns in the future.

- Exit in Time

Once you know your children are ready to take charge, make sure you exit from the business in time. Leave before you are kicked out by someone else! Now, this may not be easy for a person who has started the business from scratch. But there is no alternative to it. The best way is to give up power slowly and smoothly.

Remember, even the most iconic businessmen like Bill Gates and Narayan Murthy exited before time — although their exit did not mean 'retirement'. All they did was change their role.

And you can do that too — changing your role from running the business to mentoring it. You will be more valued and respected then.

Competition

33

Handling Competition

THE DAYS OF MONOPOLY are over. Competition is 'in'. No longer can Public Sector Units (PSU) relax, nor can traders and middle-men think that their huge profit margins will continue for long. With the world becoming a global village and technology reaching the remotest corners of each country, competition has opened up like never before.

Therefore, as new projects are started, bigger brands are launched and new markets are explored, a strategy to meet the challenges from the existing players, or future competitors, is needed. Hence, a carefully researched, planned, and calculated move is necessary in every field today. Kautilya helps us plan a strategy to handle competition.

"After ascertaining the relative strength or weakness of powers, place, time, revolts in rear, losses, expenses, gains and troubles, of himself and of the enemy, the conqueror should march ahead." (9.1.1)

Let us look at each of the aspects of the strategy, which must be evaluated before making our move in the market. Both, from one's own view point, as also from that of the competitors.

- Power

Power comes in various forms — knowledge, money, and also enthusiasm. Some of the most successful projects are the ones that are deeply studied and well-researched. Remember, the foundations are important for the structure to last.

- Place

The right place is very important. The place should be conducive for the product to sell. The right market should be found even for carrying out the experimental process. One cannot launch an agriculture based product in an urban shopping mall. The right place for it is in the rural segment.

- Time

Every product has a season — just hit it at the right time! The cold drink companies will have their marketing strategy built around the summer season. While the paint industry will advertise just before the festival season.

- Revolts in the Rear

Unknown to us there are possibilities of being stabbed in the back! Our distributors, retailers in the market as well as our very own staff can be targeted by our competitors to capture our market share.

- Loss

One should be aware of the losses that can happen in the process — not just financial, but also loss in time, material, and efforts.

- Expenses

A budget should be worked out before the whole project is started. In most cases, the budgets shoot up as the process commences. A buffer for extra and miscellaneous expenses should be considered.

- Gains (Profits)

How much is one finally going to get at the end of the whole exercise? A few projects could be one-time projects with immediate gains, while others could reap their fruits in the long-term.

- Troubles

A lot of troubles will crop up. The best way to avoid or reduce troubles is to be aware of the maximum possible problems that can arise and have a backup plan to solve them all.

Only after taking all these into account, should one march ahead to conquer the market.

34

Army and Treasury

FIRST THINGS FIRST, let us make leadership simple. Why go beating around the bush, reading a lot of books and doing various courses to understand what management and leadership really is?

Management is all about focusing on how to take your organisation forward. Even in the good old days when the concept of a company or a corporation did not exist, we had efficient managers — the ministers and the kings.

What message did Chanakya have for the leaders?

"The king brings under his sway his own party as well as the party of the enemies, by the (use of the) treasury and the army." (1.4.2)

As Chanakya pointed out, in order to control and lead an

organisation, one needs to focus on just two things — treasury and army.

- Treasury or Finance

The success of any county, state, organisation or association, is chiefly dependent on its economic and financial condition. If the balance sheet is good, cash flow is regular, profits are shown year after year and reserves and investments are in proper places, you will then be termed a financially stable firm.

So, the leader needs to make his company financially strong. Everything else will fall into place.

- Army or Manpower

The second most important aspect is the army, or the kind of men the company possesses. The more efficient, skilled and professional your employees are, the better is your productivity. The leader also needs to keep his employees from leaving his organisation.

Even in a non-profit or a voluntary organisation, including spiritual organisations, success is dependent on the number of volunteers and workers it can attract and keep.

Even though the above two seem to be different, they are interconnected. A financially strong company can easily attract better employees. And, only an efficient team can make a firm profitable.

So how does the leader achieve this? According to Chanakya. the following are some time-tested tips:

➢ Recruit the right people
➢ Invest in people — train them and pay them well
➢ Focus on developing quality in your products and services

- Keep continuous track of your finance
- Ensure that you make your company profitable

In the above sutra, Chanakya says that if these tips are followed, the King (leader) will automatically bring under his control not only his own group, but also that of his competitors.

Al Ries, a marketing strategist, wrote a book called *Focus* which includes various case studies and the analysis of successful companies.

He says, "Focus — the future of your company depends on it." Nothing beats this statement when we consider the treasury and the army.

35

Protection From Enemies

STARTING A BUSINESS, any business, is tantamount to declaring a war on the existing players. As your business grows, either of two things can happen. You may just remain another small player in the market, with steady growth. Or, the business will grow exponentially.

In the latter case, you become so big that the size you attain is one you would have never imagined in your wildest of dreams. Bill Gates, when he started Microsoft, never thought that he would become the richest man in the world and stay so for many years. Neither did Lakshmi Mittal think he would be listed among the top five in the list of richest businessmen.

Why does this happen? At a certain point, business grows at a rapid and irresistible speed — unimaginable and unthinkable.

However, like adversity, prosperity also brings its own problems — enemies.

Kautilya's Arthashastra offers advice on tackling one's enemies:

"The enemies should not come to know of his secret; he should, however, find out the weakness of the enemy. He should conceal, as a tortoise does his limbs, any limb of his own that may have become exposed." (1.15.60)

In any given industry, there are a maximum of five players at the top. Once you are amongst them, you have to be extremely alert and careful. From this point onwards, all new activities should be carried out secretively with complete detailed planning.

- Keep Your USP a Secret

Your competitive strength is all about a formula of your own making. Your USP should stay just that — your Unique Selling Point. Something special in your service or product that only you have. Keep developing those strengths. Even if the enemy knows about it, they should not be able to replicate it.

- Find the Enemy's Weakness

Be alert, very alert. You should be aware of the various moves your enemies are planning and/or making. Have a market intelligence team. You need not be the first to attack at all. But if attacked, you should know how to strike back. This would be easier if you are aware of your competitor's weaknesses.

- **Protect Yourself**

Learn to protect yourself. Just as a tortoise withdraws his limbs into its shell when threatened, you too should withdraw if someone comes to know your secrets. If the vital areas of your business are exposed, try to protect them.

But this does not mean you should always fight with your enemies. If required, one should also help one's enemies for the overall improvement of the industry. After all, competitors in the same sector form associations all the time.

Remember, the golden statement by Don Vito Corleone in the book *The Godfather* — "Never hate your enemies; it will cloud your judgment!"

36

Right Opportunity

IS SUCCESS IN BUSINESS a matter of 'luck' or 'self-effort'? It's a question often asked, especially by those who are struggling to build their companies.

There's this saying about success being 99 percent hard work and 1 percent luck. But, remember, you will never get lucky till you put in the best of your efforts. Only then will opportunity knock on your door.

Chanakya says that when such an opportunity finally comes, potentially bringing the success you aim for, you should be alert enough to grab it.

"Time comes but once to a man waiting for an opportunity; that time is difficult for that man to get again when he wants to do his work." (5.6.31)

You might have heard the adage that talks of opportunity not knocking twice, but here's another interesting one for you — "When opportunity knocks, either we are out or sleeping in!"

Still, we have to understand that it is not only about the opportunity itself but about the 'right' opportunity at that. So how does one recognise this so-called 'right opportunity'?

Here are some steps to follow, according to Chanakya:

- Nothing but the Best

Usually, people who are learning the tricks of the trade feel every opportunity is the best opportunity. This is simply not true. You will have to struggle for a few years and put in your best efforts before you develop the 'knack' to differentiate between right and wrong, good and bad, and even the simply 'better' from the very 'best'.

- Learn to Say 'No'

It's quite a temptation to say 'yes' to every event that 'seems' to be an opportunity. When an opportunity comes — stay calm. Think it through — is it a profitable venture? Plan a strategy and then decide to capitalise on it.

- Jump into It

Once you have thought it through, jump into the field right away. Do not think too much after this stage. Just go out and perform your best. You never know if such a chance will come again.

People only see the success a businessman has achieved; they never recognise the hardships that he has gone through to become successful.

Ray Kroc, the founder of Mc Donald's, was once asked in an interview, "Sir, you were very lucky! You became an overnight success." Ray remarked, "Yes, that is true. But you do not know how long the night was…!"

After putting in your time, energy, and efforts to build your dreams, do not quit when success is just right round the corner.

As Swami Vivekananda proclaimed, "Awake, arise! Stop not till thy goal is reached."

And for all this, remember, it's all a matter of timing.

37

Win-Win Policy

INDIA IS A VERY ATTRACTIVE destination for investors. The Foreign Direct Investment (FDI) coming into our country is growing day by day.

One of the ways through which we get FDI is through Joint Ventures (JV). This is where a foreign company ties up with an Indian company for business opportunities. Both of them come together to gain from the partnership.

Chanakya has a word of advice for these situations too.

He says, that for such JVs to succeed, there should be a win-win situation between the two partners:

"In a work that can be achieved with the help of an associate, he should resort to a dual policy." (7.1.18)

A dual policy means a win-win policy.

We require funds for new business opportunities. Thus, an investor becomes an associate.

Any one of the new, private insurance companies could make a perfect illustration for understanding JVs. These young insurance firms are pure joint ventures between an Indian company and a foreign one. Both came together in the field of insurance when the government opened up the sector for FDI.

The Indian partner in the JV has the experience of Indian customers. While the foreign investor is an expert in insurance. As India is a new market for the latter, it gains knowledge of the market by tying up with its Indian counterpart. The domestic firm benefits from venturing into another business field, riding high on the years of experience of its foreign backer. This is a win-win situation.

Here are some tips on how to get into successful joint ventures:

- Be Sure of Your Expertise

Your organisation should be good in one area at least. You should be an expert in that field with a proven track record.

- Make a Business Plan

Make a business plan in order to approach a possible investor for expanding your current business. Make sure that, when you approach him, it is a win-win situation. You get the investment and he gets your expertise.

- Find Like-Minded Partners

Just getting an investor does not solve your problem. Both need to trust each other and should be able to see some value addition made possible due to the partnership.

Both partners should support each other while running the business.

"Finally it's not whether we lost money in our JV that counts," said an investor, "rather, it's if we bet on the right person."

Be that right person!

38

The Winning Weapon

THINK BEFORE *THEY* THINK — that is the rule of warfare. Even in the game of chess, every move made by the opponent is studied, analysed, and carefully thought about before you make any move. If you are the first to make a move, first make a plan.

And it is this plan that needs to be protected from prying eyes. It goes without saying that businessmen should be alert. Very alert. While taking up new projects or while executing the projects in hand, a high level of secrecy should be maintained. Thus, secrecy is the most important weapon.

Chanakya advises,

"Others should not know about any work sought to be done by him. Only those who undertake it should know (about it) when

it is begun, or even when it is actually completed." (1.15.17)

What you are doing, what you are thinking, and all your moves should not be known to others. One needs to create an aura of secrecy around himself to move ahead, way ahead of the others.

In professional and powerful organisations like the Police, the Army, the Central Bureau of Investigation, till the last moment, no one knows what the next order will be. Only a handful of people work on a strictly-enforced 'need-to-know' basis and it is these people who, in turn, co-ordinate with others who are supposed to execute subsequent orders.

The call is made at the last moment and is quite sudden for those being asked to go into action. Till the moment the order is given, the seniors keep the plan entirely to themselves.

A golden rule to remember in business is that there is a big difference between planning and execution. Make your plan perfect, then execute without delay. There is no point in planning when the time has come to execute.

But let's face it — keeping secrets is tough. However, there are some tips that can help:

- Postpone

Whenever you feel like disclosing a plan to someone, remember to postpone this act.

Give yourself at least a day. Once you have done that, your self-control will improve. By practising this, you will slowly but surely get the confidence to keep things to yourself. Also, learn to observe silence for at least half an hour every day, this will enable your thoughts to rule over your talkative nature.

- Execute and Then Speak

Do not speak and then execute. It should be the other way round. The biggest danger in revealing your plans is that you give the opponent an added advantage to think before you.

- Think Ahead

On achieving success in any endeavour, we feel like talking about it to others. Rather, we feel like bragging! The best way to avoid this is to start new projects immediately. Always keep yourself busy with new plans.

Swami Shivananda, a dynamic saint and the founder of the Divine Life Society, put it best when he said, "The only way to keep yourself productive is by having at least a month's work in front of you."

Follow this advice!

39

Win the War

WHETHER IT'S IN OUR personal, or professional, life, we always face competition and hence, enemies too. We do wonder about how much stronger than us the enemy could be. Does this mean that we are going to lose the battle?

No! Chanakya never accepted defeat. However, he was practical. After all, he was an expert strategist while each person around him was playing games with one another all the while.

He believed that one must not mind losing the battle to win the war. Chanakya knew how to win over the enemy in the long run, if not immediately.

He said,

"He should seek shelter with one whose strength is superior to the strength of the enemy." (7.2.6)

The above sutra is a simple, yet excellent, gem of management, and even in real life for that matter. When faced with an enemy who is stronger than you, the best situation is to have an even stronger friend on your side.

Why does Chanakya say this?

- Strength

Former President of India A.P.J. Abdul Kalam, the missile man, once said, "Only strength will respect strength." We should be more powerful than the enemy by acquiring greater strength. If not, like Chanakya said, making friends with a much stronger ally would help counter competition.

- Experience

A stronger ally will have more experience in fighting wars. It can guide you and shelter you, even help you during calamities. When the alliance gives you advice, it is bound to be relevant because it is derived from experience.

- Long-Term Approach

One of the most important things to remember is to keep your ego in check during a battle. Do not think, for even a second, that you can win against an enemy by just sheer power. Think of the long-term, lose your ego and 'surrender' to a person superior to your enemy so that you get the required help. After all, you can defeat the enemy only if you survive through the turmoil in the long run. Battles may be lost, but the war must be won!

Win with the wisdom your superior alliance gives you, rather than losing with your personal logic.

Remember Amitabh Bachchan's dialogue in the movie *Sarkar*? *"Taakat judne se aati hai tutne se nahi."* He meant exactly what you should remember always — strength lies in making friends, not losing them.

40

Win-Win Situation

IT WAS MANAGEMENT GURU Stephen Covey who first coined the term 'win-win situation'. Now it is a commonly used terminology in the corporate world.

But what does it mean? Can there really be two winners in a game? Well, yes! It is a paradigm shift in management thinking, based on the principle of 'live and let live'.

In fact this policy of avoiding war was written by our own Chanakya:

"In war there are losses, expenses, marches away from home and hindrances." (7.2.2)

When competition sets in, and if it's not tackled carefully, both the parties can end up fighting a brutal war that causes heavy losses of time, energy, and also resources. Huge expenses are encountered when we find one party trying to outdo the other.

Now the real question is, how does one even begin to

think about 'win-win' when war is unavoidable. Think about the following points carefully:

- We All Can Share

The biggest prize in the corporate world is the market. But, remember, however hard you try, no single company can win 100 percent market share. That has never happened in the past and will never happen in the future.

So it is important to think about how one can expand the existing market, instead of thinking how much market you can capture. We can all get a bigger share, if the pie itself expands.

- All of Us Can Teach

It may sound strange, but it really is important that the business leaders should get into the teaching mode. A business leader has a lot of roles to play — teaching being one of the most important. Therefore, with years of experience that have already been earned, the top players should start teaching others.

They need to create an awareness of their own company and industry in potential markets. They should offer guest lectures in business schools, mentor youngsters in their own companies, and also chair sessions in their industry associations.

- Create More Winners

The best way to think 'win-win' is to create more winners like yourself. As some people say, "A leader is the one who can create more leaders." Invest in the 'generation-next'.

Keep looking at various sources from where you can tap potential leaders.

India Inc. today is rapidly changing. As Divya Dayal, the Vice-President (Human Resources) at a Japanese bank, Mizohu, pointed out, "In the next ten years, one of the basic problems we will face as a country is the lack of good leaders."

To tackle this scenario, many Indian corporate giants are now setting up world-class leadership and management training institutes.

This would go a long way in not only helping the industry itself, but also the markets and the entire country. After all, if India wins as a nation, all of us will be winners — the best win-win situation!

41

The Key to Success

WHILE DEVISING A CORPORATE strategy, there are certain associations and relationships that one needs to keep secret from others. And there are some that need to be discussed openly with the public. Learn to differentiate between the two.

For example, the brand ambassador of a company should be openly exhibited/used in order to achieve the desired branding and sales target. But the names of the people being used within the corporate structure — like the key technicians or consultants — should never be publicised.

Therefore, to succeed in any project the key to success is silence.

Chanakya suggests,

"In case of secret associations, those concluded in secret shall succeed." (3.1.11)

Every business leader has friends, strategists, associates and market intelligence experts from whom he takes advice and to whom he even gives information. These are his resources for thoughts. Until and unless it is required, he should never make them public. Only after understanding the importance of this, can he succeed in reaching his desired results.

Here are some steps for maintaining secrecy in a project:

- Let the Idea Evolve

Many people get excited when they come up with a 'billion-dollar' idea. They go and tell others about it. They feel they have hit on a goldmine and others will buy this idea. However, it's just a matter of time before someone else (including your competitors) takes the idea away from you and may even profit from it. So please let the idea mature in your heart and mind before you tell others about it. Give yourself time.

- Experiment Quietly

As your ideas take shape, talk to a few people — just a few who can help you make your idea practically viable. Think about all the aspects of a project that must be worked upon to achieve success — such as the research involved, finance required, the people needed, the technical expertise, time to complete the project etc. Then, before you start with the final project, do a pilot project. Thus, you will know the difficulties you are likely to encounter. Remember, a sculptor always makes a six-inch model before the actual 60-foot statue!

- Execute Effectively

You should make your moves very quietly till the time to attack comes. Most importantly, you would keep all plans hidden from your competitors. However, when you do execute the plan, make sure that it is complete and perfect. As the saying goes, "Never give your opponent a second chance; you may not survive the counter attack!"

42

Game Theory

CHANAKYA'S TREATISE *ARTHASHASTRA*, talks about one very important aspect of conducting business — the 'Game Theory'. All management personnel and economists are familiar with this, and use it very often to analyse situations and, especially competition.

Chanakya was a pioneer of the Game Theory. In *Arthashastra*, it is called the 'Mandala Theory' (Circle of Kings). It consists of various multiple permutations and combinations of dealing with the enemy, or the *Shatru*,

In a battle, when face-to-face with the *Shatru*, Chanakya says,

"If near him (enemy), he should strike in his weak point." (7.2.12)

But how does one strategise and make this move against the enemy (competitor) in today's corporate world? Some tips:

- Study the Competition

Before attacking, one should always know everything there is to know about the person or the entity that needs to be countered. Remember, war is 99 percent preparation and 1 percent execution. So, prepare well before you make your move. Accurate information should be gathered about the competitor, his plans, and objectives.

- Practise Well

Never ever go rushing into the market (or your own office, for that matter) seeking a direct conformation with the BIG guys. Gain experience first by practising well in your own region and tasks. The bigger the competitor, the more you need to prepare. In fact, it would pay to seek counsel from an experienced person. His advice can turn things around for you.

- Know the Rules of the Game

This is the most essential part! The rules of the game are the framework within which you conduct your business, or day-to-day affairs. It would be highly rewarding if you understand them well. Think about it — it's only when you have become well-acquainted with the rules that you can change them.

Just look at how the Indian hockey team was tackled. They had become invincible at the Olympics for years together. Then the competition studied the rules. They understood that the Indians were unbeatable on grass. They changed the rules of the game, and the 'turf' it is played on, literally! Since, then, even on modern-day 'Astroturfs', it continues to be a struggle for Indians.

All said and done, when the time comes to counter your competitor's moves, do not sit back. Execute. And during execution, do not strategise. The best performers have always defeated their competitors in a single move! It will work for you too.

43

Winning Over Friends and Foes

MOST OF US MUST MAKE RESOLUTIONS every new year. But do we contemplate how to better our dealings with others and be a winner in the game of life?

This is an extremely important art in today's corporate world where one should not only win and make friends, but also win over enemies.

Chanakya says,

"He should win over those of them who are friendly with conciliation and gifts, those hostile through dissensions and force." (11.1.3)

There are two categories of people each one of us has to deal with in life — friends or enemies.

- Dealing with Friends

We have to accept that friends bring sunshine into our life. Can we live without those buddies who stand by us through thick and thin? But the first rule when it comes to having a friend, is to become a good friend yourself.

According to Chanakya, the way to deal with friends is through conciliation and gifts. So, be there when they require you. The best investment in any friendship is your 'time'. Listen and guide them when they are confused and frustrated.

The other way to win friends is with gifts. No person in this world is unmoved when they receive gifts. It's human psychology to expect gifts. Always put some thought into the gift you are giving. Select something that would not only be useful, but also likable. And give it with a smile and genuine joy in your heart.

- Dealing with Enemies

It's ideal not to have enemies. But let's face facts — they are all around us, even if we do not want them. Whether in the guise of competitors, or full-blown foes, they are eternally around for us to contend with.

But the biggest problem with most of us is that we try to fight the enemy alone. This almost guarantees that you will lose the battle. You should, on the contrary, have your own team before you start the fight.

In the *Upanishads*, a student asks the teacher, "Why does the evil win?" The Guru replied, "Because the good are not united!" Once you have a strong team, it's easy to win over competition. You could even create a split in the enemy and then attack them with full force.

Whatever the case, maintain equanimity while dealing with both types. Win over yourself and then win over the others. As our scriptures say, "He who is even-minded with friend and foe is considered a wise man."

44

Respect Your Enemies

OSCAR WILDE ONCE SAID, "I choose my friends for their good looks, my acquaintances for their good characters, and my enemies for their good intellects. A man cannot be too careful in the choice of his enemies!"

The fact is that often, we do not create our enemies intentionally. But the reality is that they will exist despite us not wanting them to, whether in battle, or business.

But while we may not have a choice when it comes to choosing our enemies, we can surely choose how to deal with them. It is like playing any sport — you need to have a strategy in place to win the game with the competitor.

Chanakya also respected his enemies. His advice was,

"He should enter the enemy's residence with permission." (1.16.10)

In other words, always show respect to your enemies. Even though we may fight, let it be a 'good' fight and in the right spirit.

But how do we do this? Here are some tips to deal with your competitors and enemies:

- Never Take Them for Granted

The competitor is as intelligent as you are, if not more. So do not take him for granted. Be alert and very careful about his moves. You never know when he may attack. And you should not attack him — certainly never if you believe that he will definitely lose.

- Study Him Completely

One of the reasons for the success of the Australian cricket team is that they spend a lot of time closely studying the players of the opposite teams. They watch videos, find the weaknesses and strengths of the players they are watching. With such a perfect analysis, making a game strategy for beating the opposition becomes very easy.

- Practise, Practise, and More Practise

Just because I have a good weapon in my hand does not mean I will win the war. I should be able to use it effectively off the field before I use it in an actual war. The best warriors practise for hours every day, even in times of peace. Similarly, you should also polish your presentation, or product demonstration.

- Be Cool

Being prepared for war does not mean you should go and fight. War should always be the last option as it's destructive and expensive. Therefore, even if your competitor tries to provoke you, be calm. Never hate your enemy as it kills your ability to think logically. Even in the political field, there are 'peace' talks before the war. So give room for peace in your life as well.

It's all about being prepared like the defence force of any nation, prepared for an attack at all times. But, if war does take place, do not hesitate to fight it to the bitter end!

45

Strategy vs Tactics

STRATEGY. THIS IS THE MOST misunderstood word in today's business scenario. Many managers cannot differentiate between 'strategy' and 'tactic'. But there are some basic differences — strategy is long-term; while tactics are short term. Strategy is forward looking; tactics are situational. Strategy is vision-based, tactics are need-based.

Of course, linguistically speaking, strategy refers to the game plan for attacking and counter-attacking the enemies during war. However, it has become a core subject in the field of management and leadership. Most heads of an organisation now work on 'Strategic Management'. Still strategy is not all about warring. There is a human angle to it too. Just to illustrate this point, I will address the issue of tackling employee problems and winning their hearts.

Chanakya says,

"Strife among subjects can be averted by winning over the leaders among the subjects, or by removal of the cause of strife." (8.4.18)

Let us consider a situation where a company has gone through a lock-out due to dissatisfaction among the employees. This is reminiscent of the 1970-80s when unions used to actively represent employees.

To handle this situation, we find that Chanakya's practical three-step insight is invaluable:

- Winning Over Leaders

Every group has a leader. This leader is generally involved

in highlighting the concerns of his subjects in front of the decision-makers. It's easy to win over the whole group of subjects if you just convince the leader. However, what is important to note is whether the leader is more concerned about himself, or his people. This is where your smartness lies — to diagnose the group leader before you start negotiations.

- Remove the Cause

Even when the union used to be strong, there were companies that did not face unionism. How? Because these companies successfully solved problems even before they ever arose. I remember talking to an employee from one such organisation. He said, "Our Chairman knew our concerns even before we spoke about it. If there were genuine demands, they were fulfilled without an outsider intervening."

- Give Them 'Purpose'

One topic which management consultants love to concentrate on is 'problem analysis.' This HAS to stop! If you look for problems you will end up playing the blame game. Instead, define a purpose for your organisation and its people. Most of us are problem finders. Change this mindset and cultivate a goal-oriented approach.

As Gandhiji said, "Find a purpose, the means will follow."

Always remember — pure strategy is a road map you create to reach your purpose. Tactics are how you handle the hurdles on that road.

46

Before You Attack

THERE'S AN OLD SAYING in the army, "Your success in war depends on your preparation during peace." We are all preparing ourselves for some challenge that may crop up in the future — exams, interviews, presentations, meetings, and other such events.

But when it comes to a confrontation, we just cannot attack our enemy immediately. We have to carefully diagnose the opponent, and then decide about the attack. Sometimes, not attacking is actually the best attack!

Chankaya says,

"If there is equal advancement in peace or war, he should resort to peace." (7.2.1)

Yes, war is the last route a warrior should take. After all, it results in destruction and loss of life and assets. Even in a corporate scenario, if you are wondering whether to fight or not, evaluate the complete picture and then decide your move.

Unlike in the military, the corporate war may not result in actual bloodshed. But it does result in verbal arguments, an attack on the competitor's market, or may even end up in a courtroom and become a legal drama.

Chanakya tells us to hold on before taking such a decision. Peace is the first option. But how do we decide about an attack? Think through these lines:

- What is the Loss?

One needs to ask oneself — what loss will I suffer if I

take up the war? Apart from the monetary loss, there are other kinds of losses, such as losing time, energy, and the team's loss of morale. War is always a costly affair. As an army officer put it beautifully, "What we build in over ten years, we can lose in one day of war!"

- What is the Gain?

We also need to look at the possible gains we may get at the end of the fight — What are we fighting for? What are we going to win? Is the win really required for the benefit of one and all? Can I continue to grow without that particular gain? These deep questions need to be asked.

- The Timing

Finally, the decision to maintain peace, or to attack with all our power hinges on the right timing. This is a judgment call. The most well-equipped and trained group of people may not win the game if the timing is not right. And, on the other hand, even a small group of committed people can succeed if they make the right move at the right time.

Given this dilemma, the well-known serenity prayer could be modified, and then it would read like this — "God, grant me the ability to know when to stay quiet, the courage to attack when I must, and the wisdom to know the difference!"

47

Aspects of a Battlefield

IN BOOK 2, CHAPTER 18 OF *Arthashastra*, there is a detailed classification of the weapons used by an army.

The Armoury-In-Charge is given instructions to take care of these weapons so that the soldiers are well-equipped for a battle. The knowledge of the weapons and the skills to use them are the keys to winning a war.

What are the weapons that leaders of an organisation should have before they step into a battle? Let us look at a few important aspects:

- Knowlege and Information

Today's economy is slowly becoming a knowledge economy. The more you know and are informed about, the better equipped you are to fight. If you study various industries, you will find that the companies at the top are those that have focused on knowledge utilisation, research, and development and have also made investments in knowledge assets. This will help you plan your battle well.

- Technology

In today's shrinking world, the effective use of technology is the solution to speeding up communications and transactions. Make your organisation techno-savvy. Spend time investigating and understanding the latest technology. Use them and you will find that you have a cutting-edge over your competitors. It also reduces overheads in a big way. Many small countries that have a small population but have powerful economies have used technology for higher productivity.

- People

The man behind the machine is more important than the machine. Yes, your people, your employees, comprise your army. Without a good strong and powerful army, you can't even think of stepping into the battlefield. Not only is the size of the army important — but even the quality of the army is important. The right person for the right job! Human Resource departments have been introduced in most organisations to fulfill this need.

- Inspiration

The most important weapon you need for fighting is inspiration. If your organisation is an inspired organisation with fire in its belly, there will be a transformation in the organisation's output. If you have this quality, the first three will follow. It is the 'human will' that creates change. Small organisations with tremendous will have changed the way business is done. This is also true for certain nations. A country like Singapore, hardly the size of Mumbai, is one of the most successful economies in the world today.

As a leader, when you are preparing for the external war, first try to win your internal war. All weapons are useless, if you are not inspired to fight.

As our former President A.P.J. Abdul Kalam puts it, "It is the wings of fire that gives you the ability to reach out to the skies."

48

Partnership Among Equals

DURING THE DAYS WHEN he was creating missiles, our former President A.P.J. Abdul Kalam was asked why he was creating weapons of destruction. He replied, "Only strength will respect strength."

This is true in every aspect of life. We can only partner with people who are equal to us. We do not see any 'value-add' in the time spent with people who are lower than us in stature or knowledge.

On the other hand, if a person is above us, then that person would not see any value in us. Thus, only like-minded people belonging to the same level can bond well together.

As the saying goes, 'birds of a feather flock together'. Chanakya gives a different angle to it. He says,

"An equal should over reach, or help an equal." (7.7.15)

The concept of an equal in *Arthashastra* is that of a *Mitra*, i.e., a friend. Thus, as quoted in the above verse, you should help your Mitra and reach out to him, even before he asks for help.

There are many benefits of forging a partnership among equals:

- Better Understanding

People at the same level have a better understanding of each other — their mindsets, their thinking patterns, their approach, etc. One company's general manager, who is in-charge of leading 400 people, will easily understand the problems of another firm's general manager who is also leading a group of 400 employees. Similarly, a PhD student will understand the constraints another PhD student is facing, even if they are from different universities. That is why even marital alliances are forged between those who have an equal way of thinking, economic status, and goals.

- Synergy In Thinking

When two people of equal status come together, they are beneficial for each other. One plus one is greater than two. Alternatives get created, approaches change, you get an insight about doing things in more ways than one. As an individual, you may be small. But two small people working together as a team can beat even a bigger enemy. Bigger battles are won by having more equals on your side.

- We Grow Together

It's in our human nature to grow. But of what use is growth that's meant only for you? A rich man had once said, "I was poor, yet happy with my childhood friends. Today, I am dying a rich man without any friends." Therefore, it is important that as we grow we include our equals as part of our growth.

Remember, human life is all about partnerships. But to be a good human being, look ahead with a vision, look around to face facts, and look back to pull others along.

These are also the leadership qualities that are required if you want to lead a community, society, or nation.

49

A Safe Retreat

EMERGENCIES HAPPEN. Fire-fighting situations could crop up any time. In our highly competitive corporate world, an enemy can attack you swiftly and suddenly. One needs to be prepared for all these eventualities.

Chanakya says,

"In the absence of helpmates, he should find shelter in a fort where the enemy, even with a large army, would not cut off his food, fodder, fuel and water, and would himself meet with losses and expenses." (7.15.9)

There are times when emergencies and crises force people to run away. At such times, one needs to go to a friend or an ally who will extend a helping hand.

But, when that is not possible, one still needs to retreat into a shelter.

Chanakya gives us tips for this:

- Finding a Fort

A fort is generally a well-protected place and not just some ordinary house, or shelter. A fort has guards protecting it and will house the king in the center.

In today's corporate world, a fort would denote those places where the heads of organisations usually operate from.

Therefore, it is suggested that a king (the chairman, director, or CEO) should maintain a good relationship with many other kings (his counterparts). So that in troubled times, he can seek shelter in their fort.

- Protection From the Enemy

The enemy could be someone who is not only after you, but can also reach you. And when he realises that you are under the shelter and protection of another king in his fort, he will think twice before attacking you.

After all, battles are won not only in the battlefields alone, but also in the minds of warriors. And when you have another king on your side, you automatically gain a psychological advantage.

- Inflicting Losses in Return

When you are attacked, you can be certain that the enemy has made this move after calculating all possible losses and expenses. These calculations were relevant when you were alone, and when it was easy to grab you.

Now, when you are in the shelter of another fort and protected by a friend, it will take more effort, energy and time for the enemy to get to you. He will be forced to plan a new strategy, and consider how many soldiers he may lose himself in the process. It is a very positive situation for you, you have upped your enemy's losses.

Chanakya, a very sharp military strategist, always planned an 'exit policy' before such a situation would actually arise. So should you. In the corporate boardroom, or in the market place, or even while signing any contract, it is very important to think about the situation from all aspects and include an exit option for yourself.

50

In the Face of Competition

A LEADER'S POSITION IS AN eternally challenging one. While he has to ensure that due credit is given to everyone during good times, he also has to play the role of a motivator through bad times.

Kautilya's Arthashastra exhorts a king (leader) to ensure that his people know how to tackle the challenges he will be giving them.

Chanakya said:

"The conqueror, desirous of capturing the enemy's fortified town, should fill his own side with enthusiasm." (13.1.1)

This couldn't be more applicable in today's corporate scenario.

While India Inc. is on a roll with various mergers and acquisitions, they still need to be vigilant as they are marching ahead like conquerors out to win over their competitors — just like in a war.

They have to be aware that, before they use their employees in their onward march, inspiring them is an essential step for success.

- Understand Uncertainty

When war is declared, soldiers start speculating about their king's next move. That's because all strategies cannot be openly communicated to everyone. This naturally festers doubt in the ranks.

It is typical human nature to think negatively, rather than focus on the benefits. As a leader, you have to understand this uncertainty and think of how to take your team into confidence.

- Communicate and Inspire

Once you have your plan ready and want to communicate your intentions to your team, do it calmly and clearly. Winning your team's confidence is very important. No external motivational speaker can inspire a team the way its own leader can.

Also, it's vital your team is acquainted with the firm's vision and targets that they move in the desired manner. The added advantage of this is that employees get more inspired when their doubts are cleared.

This is essential to have optimum productivity from your team members. They will ensure you are never alone as both you and your team will have a common purpose.

- Go Forth and Conquer

It's these vision and leadership initiatives that finally make the winning moves.

Size doesn't matter, planning does. Even Chanakya talks about how guerrilla warfare tactics can help the smallest but well-inspired team take over huge armies through careful moves.

Indeed, a carefully planned strategy, an inspired team and the right leadership attitude are not only essential but also the only factors needed to win any war. But remember to share the benefits of the success with the team which helped you to get there.

51

Acquiring a Company

MERGERS AND ACQUISITIONS (M&A) are key strategies for almost all top corporations today, especially our desi ones. Indeed, India Inc. should be at the forefront of any M&A action, given that the concept was dealt with in great detail in our ancient texts.

Kautilya's Arthashastra even defines the ways of acquiring a firm:

"Acquisition is of three kinds — new, formerly possessed, and inherited." (13.5.2).

But Chanakya also made it clear that acquisition is not just mere killing and conquering. Rather, it's a well-thought out strategy which strives for the betterment of both the parties involved.

In addition to material benefits, M&As should look after the people too. If this is understood, all such processes will automatically be successful, whatever category they belong to.

- Taking Over a New Firm

In the olden days, kings used to win over new territories all the time. But they needed to do a lot of study and research since not enough was known about a strange new place.

Even today, the first step in acquiring a firm is to research it in detail. This study is usually the responsibility of a strategic planning team. Due diligence and meetings can follow only after an in-depth study.

- Taking Over an Existing Firm

More often than not, regions that were under a particular king's control are taken over by another region. This can be due to bad management, or lack of attention.

This happens in the corporate world too. When companies grow, they lose focus on their small businesses. By the time they become aware, they find that their ownership is under threat. So, the next type of acquisition is to conquer firms formerly possessed.

- Taking Over an Inheritance

A prince may have inherited a kingdom. But in due course of time, it may have been taken away from him, possibly by his own 'trusted' ministers. So when the prince matures and wants control of his inherited share, he may have to fight it out. This is acquisition of inherited property.

All those court cases you see for ownership of a small property or firm denotes this situation perfectly. Fighting back is the only way to get back what one had inherited, but lost.

Whatever the type of acquisition, having a strategic plan is a must. And more importantly than that is to provide for people on both sides of the negotiation table.

52

Where to Expand

WHILE IT'S TRUE THAT ALL companies need to expand, serious thought has to be given to where exactly they can invest. This holds true even for individuals, especially when it comes to investing in property.

Chanakya had advised:

"As between a small proximate land and a big land that is distant, the small proximate land is preferable. For, it is easy to obtain, to protect and to get rescue (oneself). The distant one is the opposite of this." (7.10.17-19)

The Tata Motors-Trinamool Congress of West Bengal

state tussle over a piece of land in 2008 brings to my mind this particular verse from Chanakya's *Arthashastra*.

In the case of the Nano plant, the Mumbai-headquartered Tatas stood to lose Rs 500 crore as they dropped their project at Singur. According to Chanakya, an alternative site for the Rs 1 lakh car should be somewhere closer to headquarters, and where local leaders are open to discussions.

So, Maharashtra or Gujarat was the best option and finally Gujarat won. Let us see why:

- Proximity

The land located nearer is always more advantageous, even if it's smaller than the far off land. That's because it's easily accessible, which makes application of decisions a lot quicker. In the case of West Bengal, it's now becoming difficult to get the concerned leaders to even come to the discussion table.

With distance being a huge disadvantage, it's difficult to find a common ground easily. Moreover, local leaders will always have a bigger say compared to any well-wishing, but external investor.

- Obtaining and Protecting

One can understand the local laws and the demands of people residing nearby more easily. Thus, it's easy to acquire and obtain. It's also easy to protect it.

Even if there is a difference of opinion, the local people and their leaders can be approached easily and discussions can reach fruitful conclusions faster.

- Rescuing Oneself

In a worst-case scenario, it's always vital to rescue oneself and the team immediately. The prime duty of a leader is to protect the safety of his subjects. Imagine the costs involved if the Tatas were to airlift their 800-strong force from West Bengal to safeguard them from local attacks.

This would be more easier and cost-effective if they were closer to the head-office based in Mumbai.

Basically, a company has to look at all such dimensions before making an investment in a new place since, in the end, success can be achieved only through a win-win situation for all.

And of course, the leadership and the local government policies also matter the most. This is the advantage that Gujarat had.

53

Peace and War

TERRORISM, BOMB BLASTS, communal riots, political protests — have become a regular part of our lives. While this is not good for any country, or even its governance, is it in anyway linked to the business community and working-class people?

Of course! The concept of 'risk management' as related to business growth is becoming an interesting field of study. But what does Chanakya have to say about it?

"For, when the gain is equal there should be peace, when unequal war is considered desirable." (7.8.34)

This is a very interesting statement that Kautilya makes —

if there is a win-win situation between two parties, we should consider peace. However, if we are only at the receiving end, war has to be considered.

Now, how do we decide if we still need peace talks, or if it's time to attack?

- Punishments Are Necessary

In addition to commerce, *Arthashastra* is also a book about law and order in society. Therefore, it is also known as *Dandaniti* (*Danda* — the rod, and *Niti* — the strategy) i.e. a book of punishments.

Only if the fear of punishments exists, will there be discipline and peace in society. No one really desires war. But, at times, it is unavoidable. 'War against terrorism' is what politicians are now talking about all around the world.

- But, Consider All Options

Chanakya's famous theory of *Sama, Dana, Danda, Bheda* comes into play here. First, try talks and discussions, not only with enemies, but also with your team members. Understand what the enemy really wants.

Also, have a dialogue with the leaders of our society — businessmen, academicians, artists, spiritual groups, media, etc. Get all of them involved and try to understand what we as a society think about it.

- Decide and Act

After all this analysis, it's important to decide the next course of action. There comes a time in every country's history when a firm decision must be taken and acted upon. Such a decision not only changes the course of history, but also decides the very survival of the nation.

During the British Raj, many believed that our colony was governed by a 'Divide and Rule' policy. Sardar Vallabhbhai Patel, our first Home Minister and Deputy Prime Minister, had a different opinion. He said, "We divide ourselves, and they rule!"

54

Tackling Terrorism

INDIA ATTACKED!
So, what's new? Ask any Indian how tired he is listening to this same news every year, it seems as if he is almost used to hearing about such terrible attacks. Most people have a fatalistic philosophy, *"Akhir ek din to marna hi hai* (after all, we all have to die one day)".

But there were also numerous disturbed readers, who sent me e-mails asking if Chanakya had suggested any solution for terrorism in the *Arthashastra*.

He had. Chanakya had said:

"Three Magistrates, all of them of rank of ministers, shall carry out suppression of criminals." (4.1.1)

This is the opening verse of Book 4 of *Kautilya's Arthashastra* on tackling ('suppression of') criminals.

- Make a Strong Policy

How many times have we observed that even the most deadly criminals manage to get away scot-free in this country? There is no fear of the law.

Therefore, the state has to adopt a much stronger law and order policy. Did you note how, after 9/11, America did not suffer from any more terrorist attacks? In our case, the attacks just grow bigger and deadlier with time.

Since 2004, we have faced as many as 16 major terrorist attacks. Why do we still need a reason to wake up? Why are we not ready to learn from our mistakes and rectify them? A strong stand against terrorism is the need of the hour.

- Study and Execute

Our ministers should study how America and other countries have tackled similar situations. They should learn from them and make an action plan. And, after doing this, it's important that they do not just sit back and do nothing.

Our ministers should learn to execute these plans. In the final showdown, the fate of the country is always in the hands of the leaders. They have to learn to be proactive.

- Get Senior Judges Together

Read what Chanakya said centuries ago — not one, but three judges should come together. Why? Because they will offer different viewpoints and perspectives. However, in the same sutra, Chanakya also advises that these 'Magistrates' should have the rank of ministers.

In the olden days, a minister was close to the king. The same situation can be replicated today by giving our law experts and judiciary more power, especially to those who have already proved the soundness of their executive powers.

As they say, "Let's work hard now so that we can sleep peacefully later."

People

55

Growing Under a Mentor

WE REQUIRE THE HELP of experienced people while undertaking various projects, or assignments. However, even though we want guidance from our seniors, we do not want them to decide how we should do our work. *Freedom* coupled with guidance is what every employee needs.

This guide can be a mentor. A mentor is an evolved leader. A leader commands, while a mentor directs. A leader is a part of the process; a mentor is a catalyst, who guides without being part of the action.

Each employee has to be nurtured with the help of a senior person who is experienced in that particular skill. This system of mentoring has taken strong roots in today's corporate training structure.

For instance, Narayan Murthy is now officially the Chief Mentor of the Infosys Group. We may have a good mentor around us. But we should know how to benefit from their company and experience. The *Arthashastra* gives us various tips on how to do this:

- Accept His Authority

"Training and discipline are acquired by accepting the authoritativeness of the teachers in the respective fields." (1.5.6)

The junior needs to have an attitude of surrender towards his mentor, his Guru. Initially, this may seem difficult for a novice brimming with ideas.

However, accepting the mentor's authority helps build discipline. The person should be able to accept that the mentor understands the subject better than he does. At times it might be difficult to accept his decisions, but he still needs to follow them. The complete picture will become clearer in due course of time.

- Constant Association

"He should have constant association with elders in learning for the sake of improving his training, since training has its root in that." (1.5.11)

Trying to associate with the mentor's thoughts, ideas, and way of thinking is very essential. This helps develop the mindset required for the job.

Being in the company of the mentor gives us a practical insight into the theories we have heard about management. The basics of any training is to improve oneself. This will happen in the presence of the mentor.

- Keep Learning and Applying

"(From) Continuous study ensures a trained intellect, from intellect (comes) practical application, (and) from practical application (results) self-possession." (1.5.16)

Finally, one has to keep applying what he has learnt from the mentor.

Continuous study helps one develop the intellect. Then he has to test his intellectual understanding by applying the lessons in practical situations. Once he sees the results, he is convinced about his knowledge. Now he has mastered the field. In fact, with the help of his mentor, the theory and practice have become one.

56

Motivating Employees

HUMAN RESOURCE DEPARTMENTS in modern corporations are focused on how to motivate the employees, or guide them to perform better and increase productivity. Chanakya uses motivational techniques in various departments of the State. Many of the methods can today be applied in the corporate world when it comes to handling employees.

Using his deep understanding of human nature, Chanakya developed a system of motivation which worked with the carrot, the stick, and many more other motivating factors. The application of his theory of motivation — *Sama, Dana, Danda,* and *Bheda* are unlimited.

- *Sama* or Consultation

This is the first step that should be taken whenever it appears that an employee is not working properly — listen to him. Have a clear understanding of his side of the story. Senior managers get information from various sources. They will get the whole picture if they listen to the information directly from the person involved.

One can discuss and suggest various solutions for the particular problem. If it is a complex problem, external experts could help.

- *Dana* or Reward

Employees work for wages and salaries. That is the key motivating factor that ensures they stay on in the organisation. The next thing is honour. Without these two kinds of encouragement, no employee will have any reason to continue working in that particular company.

Therefore, Chanakya suggests rewarding employees sufficiently in order to get work done. The reward could be in the form of incentives, paid vacations, bonuses, or promotions. Another reward would be awarding employees for their performance, such as the 'best employee award' or 'most productive person award' — a common practice in several companies today.

- *Danda* or Punishments

Many employees may not show any signs of improvement in spite of constant prodding and various other efforts. Neither rewards nor incentives will bring them out of their lethargic state. This is a serious situation. If not corrected, a sense of complacency can spread through the whole organisation.

Therefore, Chanakya recommends a stronger step — punishments. A rap can be subtle or gross, depending on the person as well as the situation that warranted it. It can be a warning, a suspension, a cut in salary, or even a demotion.

- *Bheda* or Split

Though this is not encouraged at all, it is the final step. When none of the other methods work, it is concluded that the organisation and the employee cannot work together any further. It is best to part ways for the benefit of both.

If it is a large organisation that can bear the financial expense of that particular employee, he can perhaps be transferred to a department where his productivity will not be a major issue. In smaller firms, or employee-productivity-oriented organisations, he must be asked to leave.

57

Bidding Goodbye to Employees

THE SKILLED MANPOWER is increasing in our country, the competition for hiring better employees is growing at an unprecedented rate among companies, the attrition rate is going up, and the challenge of retaining your able force is increasing. This is the scenario in almost all sectors of the economy. Every entrepreneur is thinking about and forming strategies to tackle such incidents.

During such a phase in any industry, Chanakya, says,

"Masters may bear testimony for servants, priests and preceptors for disciples, and parents for sons." (3.11.32)

If your subordinate is leaving the organisation for better prospects and you are not able to provide them with the same benefits, it is the duty of a senior to offer his best wishes to the junior and say goodbye.

The above verse says that the master should also provide certificates (testimony) and reference. Let him prosper in his life — is what you should feel for that individual.

However, such parting of ways is not very easy to accept. How can we make such moves in life more positive and happy, for both parties?

Tips for Employees Leaving the Organisation:

- Give Advance Notice

Every company has a minimum notice period. Make it a point to fulfill that agreement and do not just run away. Speak to your boss and make him understand why you are leaving.

- Replace Yourself

When you leave, the biggest question for a boss is — who is going to do your work? The best solution is to have an alternative ready. Even you can look for potential people and bring them to your boss's attention.

- Train Another New Person

The best way to tackle this situation is to get a person trained to do your work before your last day.

Tips For Employers:

- Accept Reality

People will leave and you must accept this important fact. Do not expect that someone will be devoted to you all their life.

- Continuous Training

Keep recruiting and training people on a regular basis. If you have a requirement of 50 people, train 75-100 people as ready backup.

- Multi-Tasking

Teach all employees how to perform multiple processes. So, when someone leaves, you can immediately ask others to take up his task.

Chanakya suggests that no employer should let his

employee leave after a fight and with hard feelings. You never know when you will require the person again.

In *Mahabharata* we find this pearl of wisdom — "Life is alike logs of wood flowing in a river, they flow together for some time and part, and meet again."

So, you never know when time will bring your old acquaintances back in your life.

58

Managers into Leaders

HUMAN CAPITAL, INTELLECTUAL CAPITAL, human resource — these are terms used to define the value of people in any organisation. These days, every organisation is focusing more and more on these aspects. Today, a company's ROI (Return on Investment), productivity, as well as profits in all areas, are based on the quality of people it has.

An organisation may have good manpower in terms of numbers. But, if these people are not fully productive, or not working to their optimum potential, the organisation is at a loss.

The first challenge for any organisation is to get good people. The next challenge is to train those good people into becoming good leaders.

On this Chanakya says,

"When he (prince) is ready for it (knowledge), experts should train him." (1.17.27)

When the HR Department is recruiting people from business schools, or even from other companies, they are initially looking for good managers. But if the company has to scale up, the next challenge is to make them great leaders. Even in the above verse, Chanakya calls for the identification of potential leaders and then for providing them with leadership training. But how do we understand if a manager, or an employee, is a potential leader?

Here are some tips:

- Leadership is a Mindset

Leadership is not a position or a designation. It is a way of thinking — a mindset. Therefore, a business leader has to keep an eye on the quality of the minds of his people. A leadership mind is a great mind. It is continuously learning. It does not get stuck when it sees a problem. It will seek alternatives and find different methods to get out of it. It challenges itself.

- Solution-Focused

A potential leader is solution-focused. Once, I was conducting a training programme which dealt with the topic, 'From good managers to great leaders'. A delegate asked me, "My boss is always the decision-maker. He usually brings the solution. Then why should I not just go to him with problems?"

I said, "Yes you are right. You have to present the problem to him. But go to him with two or three alternative solutions. Let the boss decide which solution is best for the organisation. But the thinking *also* has to be done by you, not only your boss!" *Think solutions* — is the mantra for success.

- Implementation

Most managers are good planners, but bad implementers. The difference between a manager and a leader is this implementation aspect. Just do it. At times, you do make mistakes, but learn from the mistake and move on in life.

59

Delegating Work

LOOK AT ANY ORGANISATION AND you are bound to find a boss who is frustrated with his subordinates. While a junior can be blamed for non-productivity to some extent, most of the problems are caused by the leader himself, due to improper delegation of work.

In *Arthashastra*, Chanakya had included a chapter on the 'Training of elephants'. He said:

"In conformity with the appearance, he should give exercise to the gentle and the dull (elephant), and to the animal with mixed characteristics, in various types of work, or in accordance with the season." (2.31.18)

So, Chanakya calls for identifying potential candidates as per their (an elephant in this case) nature and even according to the different seasons, as it may affect the way they work.

In human terms, we can understand how much thought goes into choosing the 'right person for the right job'. After all, a mistake at this stage can result in real frustration in the long run.

But how does one do this?

- Evaluate People

This is the first step for effectively carrying out what is called man-management. Many bosses fail to do this. When an interview is conducted, a well-written CV or resume can impress everyone. Even the answers and opinions revealed during the interview will help you realise if the candidate is promising.

But, there is a big difference between promises and the actual delivery of work. Give yourself time before passing any kind of judgment on anyone. Always observe and study a person for a minimum of three months (that's what training periods are for).

Watch them closely and observe their strengths and weaknesses. You will get a better grasp of the person's nature, behaviour, and potential output.

- Different Situations

A person who is very successful in one venture may not be successful if asked to handle a different situation. Even the most successful salesman may fail when it comes to selling a different product, or in a different region.

So, understand that each person's output is not guaranteed forever. Different situations and circumstances can change a person's productivity and even performance. And you have to identify these traits.

- Different Timings

Next, you really need to understand how a person's output changes at different times. For example, students generally learn much better if they study during the early morning. That's simply because the mind tends to become lazy later on in the day and hence, memorising information requires less effort in the morning.

Chanakya referred to this as 'seasons'. So find out what are the best productive times for your subordinates and allocate work "...in accordance with the season!"

All successful businessmen and leaders know the art of delegating work. If you want to be a successful man-manager too, then thinking, planning, studying, and experimenting with human psychology will become essential.

60

Protecting Old Employees

LOOK AT ANY BUSINESS ORGANISATION which is over 20 years old and you will find that it has two generations working there. Both these generations have different mindsets and attitudes.

While the younger generation has great opportunities and switches jobs very easily, the older generation is more committed and steady.

We see a similar dichotomy in today's urban-rural divide in India, wherein the urban residents are inherently restless and on-the-move, while the rural denizens are more sedate and satisfied with life.

Chanakya had a suggestion for employers who want to create appropriate policies for both:

"He (leader) should grant safety to the countryside as it may have been settled." (13.4.2)

In the olden days, kings had to think deeply before taking any decision that would have affected people residing in the villages. Providing safety and security was of paramount importance, as residents of those particular places did not want to shift easily. Similarly, the older generation in any organisation must also be taken care of.

They are committed and set in that one place (organisation). To the leader of such organisations, Chanakya suggests that instead of trying to alter their job profiles — provide them with safety.

But how do we deal with the older employees in an organisation?

- Benefit From Their Experience

Experienced people are valuable assets for any organisation as they have put in a lot of hard work to support and build it.

Never take them for granted as they prove to be useful in the most difficult of times. The best utilisation of senior employees in a company is to make them train the younger ones and the new entrants with their rich experience. This has the added advantage of creating mutual respect between the two generations within the organisation, and will also be in accordance with Chanakya's advice to a prince — "Meet elders and learn from them."

- Change Them, but Slowly

Change is a fact of life. And while the younger generation is quick and ready to change, the elders may resist it. So, even though it's important and a must, give the senior employees more time to change.

In addition to older employees, this patient approach will

also benefit the overall company as the most successful organisations are the ones that understand that the path to success is led by the maturity of the seniors coupled with the dynamism of the youth.

To Avoid

61

What a Leader Should Not Do — 1

ARTHASHASTRA IS NOT ONLY a compilation of Chanakya's wisdom, but also contains practical insights into even more ancient lessons of management, politics, and strategy.

Arthashastra contains a wealth of wisdom on leadership, its development, and application. There is some valuable information about the challenges of leadership, something that today's corporate world is struggling to understand. Chanakya not only tells us what a leader should do, but also what he should 'not' do.

In Book 7, Chapter 5, from verse 19 to 26, Chanakya outlines 21 things that a leader should avoid doing. We will be studying these words of caution in the next ten chapters. These can be applied not only to business leaders, but also to heads of departments, project leaders, community leaders, politicians, and can even be applied by the head of a family, or any other institution, or organisation.

Chanakya had said,

"Reasons for dissatisfaction of subjects: discarding the good and favouring the wicked." (7.5.19-26)

Who are the subjects?

Well, they are the people who are reporting to you, or are dependent on you. They wait for your directions, which in itself has a direct effect on their lives. In the case of a company, it's the employees. In a department, they are your team members. In a family, they are your children and relatives. The first and foremost duty of a king (leader) is to keep his subjects happy.

Now, the first reason for subjects to become unhappy is when the king discards the good and favours the wicked. Subjects come to the leader for justice. When they do not find a solution to their problems among themselves, they seek the leader's advice, direction, and justice. If he favours the wrong and discards the right, this is a very serious problem.

Here are some tips on how to understand who is right:

- Listen to Both Together and Separetely

It's very necessary to listen to both sides of a story. But after the two parties have expressed their views together, do not hurry with your decision. When both parties are facing each other, there are a lot of emotions and personal feelings expressed. Therefore, listen to them separately too. Get the facts. You will get a better idea of who was right. At times we are not able to come to any decision, this is called 'Dharmasankath'. In such conflicting situations take the help of books (scriptures) and masters learned in the particular field.

- Announce the Verdict Unemotionally

After you have analysed the situation, announce your verdict. Also explain the 'reason' behind the conclusion you have reached. Be just. But more than anything else, be unemotional. That's the most vital part.

The whole idea is not to hate the bad. As Gandhiji put it, "Remove the wickedness, not the wicked." Even while punishing the wrong, one should give them an opportunity to learn and improve.

62

What a Leader Should Not Do — 2

AMONG THE MANY THINGS that a leader should avoid doing, Chanakya says,

"Reasons for dissatisfaction of subjects: By starting unrighteous injuries not current before, by indulgence in impiety and suppression of piety, by doing acts that ought not to be done." (7.5.19-26)

These three actions could alienate a leader from his subjects. First, if a leader starts harming others in a way that was not used before. Second, by indulging in wicked deeds and suppressing good deeds. Third, by performing actions that should be avoided.

How does the leader know if his behaviour and actions are right? Here are some tips:

- Do Not Start New Punishments

In every company or organisation, there are methods of punishing the wrongdoer. For example, warnings and memos are issued. At times, employees are even suspended. But note that these are within the laws of the company. Never ever try to do any serious injury that goes beyond the law. For example, never slap or hit an employee in front of others, even for a serious lapse, or bad behaviour. After all, this is not only a physical injury, but also an emotional injury. Punishments within the right limit are always respected and honoured.

- Be a Person of Character

We find that many leaders are hypocrites. They show a very different face in front of their employees, while their private life is generally not very ideal. As it is said, "The character of a man is what he is in the dark." So a leader, even in his non-public life, should remain a man of great integrity. Be truthful to yourself.

- Differentiate between 'Right' and 'Wrong'

This is the greatest quality that a leader can develop. While running an organisation or company, there are times when the leader comes across conflicting situations. Sensitive issues like money, people management, etc become his regular concerns. If he cannot differentiate between what to agree and what to disagree with, he will always be stuck. To master this art, learn from those who are far more experienced, or others whom we call 'men of wisdom'.

Always, remember that the well-known serenity prayer of Reinhold Niebuhr also applies to a leader when he walks into an office:

"God grant me the serenity to accept the things I cannot change; courage to change the things I can; and wisdom to know the difference!"

63

What a Leader Should Not Do — 3

A LEADER SHOULD BE very alert and vigilant about his own actions. Chanakya points out,

"Reasons for dissatisfaction of subjects: By ruining rightful acts, by not giving what ought to be given and securing what ought not to be given to him (the leader)." (7.5.19-26)

There are leaders who try to suppress the good deeds performed by others. For example, if there are any projects or ideas that have been worked upon by the subordinates, they should not be destroyed. Rather they should be preserved and considered as an asset to the organisation.

Next, what rightfully belongs to the subjects should be given to them — be it their salaries, incentives, or promotions. Even a pat on the back is a great reward for juniors.

Finally, the leader should not try to get for himself that which he does not deserve. He should only take his due share.

Here are some tips:

- Encourage New Ideas

Your employees are not just machines to be operated. They are human beings with a head on their shoulders. Each mind can create a different idea, and new ideas are the fuel of any organisation. As a leader, it is very important to keep note of these new ideas and experiment with them.

While doing this, involve the employee who came up with that particular idea. Also give credit to him/her.

- Honour and Respect Them

A psychologist once said, "Like food, shelter and clothing, *appreciation*, is a basic human need too." So learn to appreciate every person. A good word from the boss goes a long way in boosting employee morale.

And this should not be artificial. Show that you genuinely respect them. In many companies, there are 'employee of the month' awards and in some organisations, a photo of the most efficient employee is displayed at the reception.

- Never Misuse Your Power

Remember the famous dialogue from the movie *Spiderman* — Peter Parker receives sage advice from his uncle, "With great power comes great responsibilities!" A leader can misuse the power, if he is not a person of integrity. Especially if he is not answerable to anyone. However, he should make himself accountable to himself. Additionally, see to it that others get equal opportunities to become good leaders themselves. A good leader is the one who creates more leaders.

In the Navy, when the ship crosses the equator, a ceremony called 'Crossing the Line' is held. During this, a junior cadet is made the captain of the ship and all the senior officers have to follow his orders. Try this for a day in your organisation. While this may sound like fun, you will also learn a lot about what your juniors think about you.

64

What a Leader Should Not Do — 4

LEADERSHIP IS A VERY DYNAMIC responsibility. It's not something to be learnt from books or lectures alone. Rather, it's about various factors that one needs to tackle in any given situation.

Continuing this series on Chanakya's tips for effective leadership, we find that he repeatedly emphasises the importance of leading by example. The next two points tell us what makes a bad leader:

> "Reasons for dissatisfaction of subjects: By not punishing those deserving to be punished; by punishing those not deserving to be punished." (7.5.19-26)

In the movie *Troy*, an officer tells the General, "Sir, the army is under fear that you may punish them." The General adds something very important, "Fear can be constructive if you can manage it well."

Men are managed by the fear of punishment. It is because of the fear of the police, that the crime rate is controlled. It is because of the fear of losing the job that employees become productive. It is only because of the fear of punishment that children are controlled by teachers and parents.

However, managing someone's fear is an art.

Here are some tips on managing fear:

- Be Fearless Yourself

It is easier said than done. Being fearless at all times is the highest human achievement. Only years of doing the right things can make one totally fearless. A warrior once said, "If I look directly into the eyes of the enemy for a few moments, my fear disappears." In other words, face the challenges of life directly without depending on anything or anyone.

- Never Misuse Fear

Leaders can misuse the fear of their subordinates. One naturally commands respect just because of being in a position of power. Still, respect cannot be demanded. One can force others to respect them through authority and the power wielded. But to earn respect, you have to win the head and the heart of the other person. If you want to check if you are a successful leader or not, try to understand if every one is comfortable and happy when you are around.

- Punish Fairly

At times, punishment is unavoidable. However, one can punish rightly and justly. If you punish too much, you will be seen as a terror. But if you are too soft, the work will not get done. It's a balancing act. So think twice before you pass your judgment — be firm, yet considerate.

A criminal was being sent to the gallows. He was asked what his last wish was. He replied to the shock of the jailor, "To kill my father because of whom I am going to the gallows…" he continued, "He never corrected me when I was wrong, nor did he punish me when I deserved it."

65

What a Leader Should Not Do — 5

CONTROLLING CRIME IS AN extremely vital function in any society. By not arresting criminals, the police not only gives support to existing criminals, but also encourages new criminals. On the other hand, if the police arrests someone who should not be arrested, a new criminal is created.

A leader should be aware of this truth, since such a situation can easily arise in any corporate.

Hence, Chanakya says,

"Reasons for dissatisfaction of subjects: By seizing those who ought not to be seized; by not arresting those who ought to be seized." (7.5.19-26)

The classic book by Victor Hugo, *Les Miserables*, brings this out in a very dramatic manner. A man gets arrested for stealing a loaf of bread under unavoidable circumstances and is put into prison for over twenty years, and from a noble man a criminal is born.

While taking any decision, the leader should carefully consider this aspect. But how will he wipe out crime and still be just? Here are some tips:

- Understand What Causes Crime

There are two reasons why a person becomes a criminal — one is need, and the other is greed. When a truly needy person cannot fulfill his basic needs, he takes the easy route of crime. Food, clothing, shelter, and financial security are basic needs. If these are not provided, there is a high risk that the person will take to theft and robbery. A leader should have complete knowledge of his subordinate's basic requirements. He should even go that extra mile to make sure that even the employee's families are taken care of.

- Control Greed

The second reason for a person to take to a life of crime is greed. In spite of their high standard of living, many people from rich families turn to crime. In such cases, the leader has to enforce the fear of punishment. If not punished, they can take the law for granted. "Arrest them," says Chanakya. Once given a loose hand, it is difficult to control them later. When one such powerful person is punished, automatically the others come under control.

- Make and Apply a System

The only way to keep crime under control is to make systems that are beneficial to the law and order of any state or organisation. However, just making systems is not helpful — they need to be applied properly. The law should not stay in the books alone. Rather, it should be used to maintain social order.

Always remember that you cannot support a criminal even if he is someone known to you.

As a thinker once said, "If you share your friend's crime, you make it your own."

66

What a Leader Should Not Do — 6

A LEADER IS A PROTECTOR. He can be compared to a shield that saves the subjects from external enemies. But, what would happen if the protector himself became the destroyer?

Consider Chanakya's words seriously, or expect your subjects to feel insecure.

He says,

"Reasons for dissatisfaction of subjects: By doing harmful things and destroying beneficial things, by failing to protect from thieves and by robbing (them) himself." (7.5.19-26)

First and foremost, a leader should not do anything that will harm people or the organisation. Also, beneficial things should not be destroyed. For example, destroying respected religious symbols can lead to problems.

Secondly, a leader should protect the subjects from robbers or any other external factors that can erode the wealth of the people, the state, or the employees of an organisation. Most importantly, he should not rob them himself!

But how can a leader ensure such protection? Here are some tips:

- Be the Wall

The leader has to be like a wall — a protection as well as a barrier. When an outsider tries to attack your subordinates, step in front of them and face the challenge yourself. An employee may not know how to take care of himself. In such situations, the mighty leader is his/her only hope. So be there when they need you.

- Take Action Against Outsiders

"Any one who disturbs the happiness and the peace of my subjects will not be spared!" said a king. Similarly, as is indicated in the verse, Chanakya says that the king should protect the subjects from thieves. If a thief is caught, punish him immediately. If he is left free, the fear of the thief returning lingers in the minds of all. Strict actions will ensure the people's confidence in the leader.

- Don't Rob Your Own People

Robbing does not just mean stealing money and other physical objects. Honour, dignity, and gratitude can be stolen as well. If a person truly deserves it, then give him rewards and awards. Your people are your greatest assets. Pay them well, pay them on time. Remember, only if your own army is strong will it fight for you.

A leader also has to be a good fighter. And when he has to fight for his people he needs to do his very best. As Faye Wattleton said so beautifully, "Whoever is providing leadership needs to be as fresh and thoughtful and as reflective as possible to make the very best fight."

67

What a Leader Should Not Do — 7

HIGH ATTRITION RATES ARE a major problem in the IT, ITeS, BPO, and other sectors. The reasons why people leave a job could be anything — the lack of incentives, or better offers from rival companies who are luring away the employees to deal with their own shortage of manpower.

But regardless of such external conditions that the current employers can hardly do anything about, the fact remains that employees are motivated or demotivated by the way their employers treat them.

There are three ways of getting work done from your subordinates — instigation, motivation, and inspiration. Instigation is the way terrorists are made to work. Motivation involves incentives and promotions, whereas inspiration comes from within the self, which is eternal and everlasting.

The real challenge for an employer is to take his employees from 'Motivation to Inspiration'.

Chanakya outlines the reasons that demoralise employees,

"Reasons for dissatisfaction of subjects: By ruining human exertions, by spoiling the excellence of work done." (7.5.19-26)

Employees work hard and exert themselves. If their efforts are not recognised and are destroyed instead, the first seed of attrition is sown. Secondly, when the employees create or produce something better for the company, he or she deserves rewards. So, how does one inspire one's employees?

- Money is the Priority

Do employees work for money? Yes, they do. That is the first and the most important requirement. No organisation can keep a person inspired, if the salaries are not paid on time. Also offer options beyond their salaries — employee stock options, incentives, shares in profits, and other schemes can be worked out by the management to keep the employees financially secure.

- Work Hard, Rest Well

The employer has to believe that optimum productivity is achieved by giving space and peace of mind to the employee. In some developed countries, employees work very hard for ten months to take a two-month vacation. We may have a problem with this model, but the important fact is that the thought of a two-month vacation has made the employee work hard for ten months. The balance between work and rest has to be maintained for better results.

- A 'Higher Purpose'

Employees want something beyond money and that is respect and challenge. They also want a purpose for their lives. If the leader is able to find that 'purpose' for the employees then phenomenal success is guaranteed. This is a spiritual requirement. The Spiritual Quotient (SQ) of the employee has to be developed for this to happen.

A recruitment advertisement of a well known IT company carried a caption under an employee's photograph: 'I found a purpose to live for in this organisation'. A 'Best Employer' survey has also found 'higher purpose' to be essential for employees.

68

What a Leader Should Not Do — 8

DURING ONE OF MY TRAINING programmes, while discussing the leadership qualities described by Chanakya, a participant observed, "It would have sounded more positive if the session was called 'What a leader should do'."

I explained that the title of the session which emphasised what leaders should *not do* was by design, rather than by fault. The human mind works in a certain pattern and studies reveal that we become more alert when we hear negative words.

Words such as 'danger', 'death' and 'destruction' have the power to move a person from lethargy to activity. So continuing this ten-part series, we now look at a few more things a leader should *not* do...

"Reasons for dissatisfaction of subjects: By doing harm to principal men and dishonouring those worthy of honour, by opposing the elders, by partiality and falsehood." (7.5.19-26)

In the above verses, the emphasis is on three key ideas — respect for elders, being impartial, and not engaging in falsehood.

- Respecting Elders and Principal Men

A society which does not respect elders and men of knowledge cannot survive for long. The Sanskrit word for elders is *'Vriddha'*. The word 'elder' here has two meanings: one, a person who is elder by age, and second, a person who is elder by wisdom. It is natural to respect any person who is elder to us by age. We find that, across Asian cultures, respecting elders has been considered a noble and high virtue. However, there are young people with a lot of knowledge or wisdom who also command respect. Even they are *Vriddhas*.

One of the reasons why young managers from top business schools land high salaries and top positions is the knowledge they bring into the company. Such young, but senior, people should always be respected and never dishonoured. Do not oppose them. Listen to their views before taking any decision.

- Not Being Partial

In conflict management, the best thing to do is to do what is 'correct'. Do not favour those who are wrong even if they are the people closest to you. On the other hand, always support those who are right, even if they are not known to you. Partiality demoralises everyone in an organisation. So be even-minded, and take an objective view before making any move.

- Not Indulging in Falsehood

Satyameva Jayate, says the Indian national emblem. But almost everyone thinks this cannot be practised in today's world. This is not true. The reality is that we do not have patience to wait. All the top companies that practise good governance look for long-term benefits. Focusing on research and development, people, strategy over tactics, etc., are key aspects of success for such organisations. Therefore, you should also not support falsehood.

69

What a Leader Should Not Do — 9

A MANAGEMENT STUDENT ONCE asked me, "Do businessmen think only of money all the time?" I replied, "The answer to this is very subjective, however there are many other things that the businessman needs to think through, even for making money. Being financially successful — which is a basic requirement — is determined by other parameters like goodwill, service levels, and also commitment from your very own people."

Now, we will look at some more factors highlighted by Chanakya that a leader should be alert about:

"Reasons for dissatisfaction of subjects: By not requiting what is done, by not carrying out what is settled." (7.5.19-26)

In other words, a businessman also has to think about his subordinates who become unhappy when they are not paid for what they have done and, secondly, when their leader becomes complacent.

- Not Paying for What is Done

The economic cycle of a business is dependent on cash flow from one person to other. The client pays for the service to the provider; they in turn pay their employees and suppliers. The suppliers will have to pay their suppliers. Even if one link in the chain breaks, there will be disharmony. Therefore, a leader needs to pay his dues to everyone *on time*. After completing a job, always pay the people involved.

- Not Being Complacent

An entrepreneur started a business and struggled a lot. Finally, his business became financially successful. He then went to his mentor and asked, "Sir, now my business is doing well. What should I do?" The mentor advised, "Go start another business."

This is where the real fun begins. The spirit of being industrious needs to be carried forward. After having learnt all about how to start and run a business, one should never become complacent.

In fact, use your know-how to start other businesses and projects. Till this point, you required a mentor. Now you can become a mentor to other struggling businessmen.

- Continuing What You Have Started

Starting another business does not mean that you must stop your first venture. From being a person who worked on the specific details of the first business, you can now move on to a supervisory level. You still need to drive the sales of the first business, but adopt a holistic approach. Your time will be spent between the first and the new business you have started. Manage both with equal commitment.

I was acting as a consultant for one of India's biggest conglomerates. As we were discussing strategies, the director told me, "For us, it is not about just running a business. We are in the business of running businesses!"

That is how great businessmen think!

70

What a Leader Should Not Do — 10

AN EMPLOYEE'S HAPPINESS or unhappiness is purely in the hands of the leader. With this, we come to the last two notes of caution for leaders.

Chanakya continues,

"By the negligence and indolence of the king and because of the destruction of well-being (through these causes) decline, greed and disaffection are produced in the subjects." (7.5.19-26)

A leader should never be careless. Even a small issue should not go unnoticed. Secondly, the employee's prosperity and well-being should never be disturbed. If a leader ignores this advice, the downfall of the organisation begins.

The primary reason why leaders tend to be negligent and indolent is lethargy. Without vision, greed takes over. The organisation begins to break apart.

Throughout this series of ten chapters (Chps 61-70), the one clear message is — 'Be Alert'. Keep watch over others and also over yourself. Some tips on being alert:

- Be in Touch with the Last Man

The challenge for any government is to check if the last man in the last village is happy. Till that is achieved, a leader's work is not complete. At times, we find that what is reported is only the success of a few people. As a leader, never go by these reports. Be on the 'ground' yourself. Regularly track what even the peon or driver feels. Talk with them, understand what keeps them going, or makes them feel frustrated. Take corrective steps.

- Take Time Out without a Reason

In the corporate world most of the work done is based on agendas, results and targets. It's important to open up your mind. It gives a fresh outlook to the organisation. There should be at least a small part of your day when you do nothing! The space that this creates in your mind will give a new insight into the work one does. With that insight apply new techniques.

- Keep Watch

Keep an eye over the people. Keep watch on what is happening in the industry. Keep a watch on changes in the surroundings and your society. All things in the world are interconnected. A small change in some other place will affect you soon, in some way or the other. Therefore, keep yourself updated and informed in all matters.

In this 10-part series we dealt with 21 points that a leader should avoid doing. A student once said to me, "Sir, this is very difficult to follow as I can't remember so many points."

Well, one does not have to remember them all. If you practise even one of these rules, the remaining will follow. They are interconnected. Just start. That is the only way to be sure if these techniques work.

Good luck on the journey to discover the leader in you…